Every Day with Jesus

JAN/FEB 2018

Pursuing God

'show me your glory.'
Exodus 33:18

Selwyn Hughes
Revised and updated by Mick Brooks

© CWR 2017. Dated text previously published as *Every Day with Jesus: Going Deeper with God* (January/February 1995) by CWR. This edition revised and updated for 2018 by Mick Brooks.

CWR, Waverley Abbey House, Waverley Lane, Farnham, Surrey GU9 8EP, UK **Tel: 01252 784700**
Email: mail@cwr.org.uk Registered Charity No. 294387. Registered Limited Company No. 1990308.

Cover image: Istiaque Emon
Quiet Time image: Ray Hennessey
Printed in England by Linney

MIX
Paper from responsible sources
FSC® C015900
www.fsc.org

A word of introduction...

At the start of a new year, this new beginning, what could be a greater goal than the pursuit of God?

Thinking of new beginnings, who would've thought that – like the small boy who offered up his loaves and fishes to Jesus – God would use a few thoughts on the back of a postcard and multiply them in such a wonderful way that they would become this much-loved publication? Originally, *Every Day with Jesus* was given away free to those who promised to pray daily for revival. Inside the front cover was printed the words: 'an aid to personal revival'.

As I have reflected on these daily Bible reading notes, I am increasingly convinced that they are so much more than a daily devotional – a series of punctuated moments at the beginning or end of each day. *Every Day with Jesus* points us to our original design and the way in which God wants us to live our lives every day: it's a lifestyle.

So it's my prayer that, whatever lies in store this year, each of us will know what it is to live, breathe and walk every day with Jesus.

Throughout this issue, there are special pages highlighting the different areas of CWR's work and what we can offer you in your pursuit of God. Do visit our website for more information.

Grace and peace,

Mick

Mick Brooks, Consulting Editor

Free small group resource to accompany this issue can be found at **www.cwr.org.uk/extra**

f The *EDWJ* Facebook community is growing!
To join the conversation visit **www.facebook.com/edwjpage**

No fixed rate

'But grow in the grace and knowledge of our Lord and Saviour Jesus Christ.' (v18)

We begin a new year exploring some of the possible steps we need to know and can take to pursue God and gain a deeper and more intimate relationship with Him. One of the questions put to me most often during my years spent as a minister and a counsellor is this: 'Why does one person seem to have a closer relationship with God than another, even though both have been on the Christian way for the same length of time?' Even the most casual observer of the Christian life cannot help but notice that people do not travel along the road at the same rate. We all grow older at the same rate! A year is just as long for someone in their twenties as it is for someone in their seventies. But wisdom and intimacy with God does not, it seems, happen at a fixed rate.

From time to time I have met Christians who have been on the road of discipleship for fewer years than I have, yet they seem to know God more profoundly. They leave me feeling seriously challenged and humbled. Is this something you too have experienced? You might meet people who, though younger than you in terms of discipleship, are able to forgive injuries more readily than you; they might seem to be free of cynicism that you may sometimes struggle with, and are swift to praise others who they see doing well in the things they want to do themselves. What freedom! How are they able to live this way?

This is the issue that we will explore over the opening weeks of this new year. The Scriptures leave no doubt that God wants to move closer to us. The question we have to ask ourselves is: Do we want to move closer to Him?

FURTHER STUDY

1 Cor. 3:1; 14:20; Eph. 4:1–14

1. How does Paul describe the Corinthians?

2. What was Paul's desire for the Ephesians?

Father, I answer this question with a resounding 'Yes'. I know, however, that before I can change, I must be challenged. So challenge me and change me. In Christ's name I pray. Amen.

A crucial element

FOR READING & MEDITATION – ACTS 17:16–34

'but now [God] commands all people everywhere to repent.' (v30)

We continue considering the question: Why do some travel along the road of discipleship quite slowly, while others appear to cover twice the distance in half the time? There are many reasons why this might be so, but let's consider the way in which we begin the Christian life.

Those who have looked closely at how people come to make a commitment to follow Jesus tell us there are two main ways of coming to faith in Christ. One is through a dramatic conversion, whereby a person is confronted with the claims of Jesus and makes a decision to follow Him in a single moment. The other is when a person moves more slowly into faith, and sometimes cannot even pinpoint the exact moment when he or she made their life-changing commitment. Let's remember that both experiences are real and valid. In previous issues I have often said that the best evidence that we are alive is not our birth certificate, but the fact we are going about our daily lives as living, breathing people. I find no problem when individuals say they do not know the day or hour when they committed themselves to Jesus. The truth is revealed in their daily life, and their pursuit of the ways and character of God the Father are outworked in prayer, engaging with God's Word and gathering with the community of Christians.

FURTHER STUDY

Acts 3:11–20;
Luke 13:3;
Acts 26:19–23

1. What was Peter's message to the onlookers?

2. How important is repentance?

The reality is that no matter how one enters the Christian life – suddenly or slowly – the most essential element is repentance. I have no hesitation in saying that if we do not understand what is involved in living repentant lives, then regardless of how we start the Christian life, there will be no serious progress.

My Father and my God, if repentance is so important – and I believe that it is – then help me understand it more deeply. Teach me dear Lord. In Jesus' name I ask it. Amen.

A change of mind

FOR READING & MEDITATION – 2 TIMOTHY 1:1–12

*'your sincere faith, which first lived in your grandmother Lois
and in your mother Eunice' (v5)*

Yesterday we explored two main types of entry into the Christian life – dramatic and arresting, or a more gradual growth and awareness of the presence of God. Paul the apostle had one of the most dramatic conversions, yet his disciple Timothy does not seem to have had a similar experience. We cannot be sure, but Timothy's coming to faith, a process apparently greatly influenced by his grandmother and mother, seems to have been much slower. We said also (and some may have found this surprising) that without a clear understanding of repentance, there can be no serious progress and deepening in the Christian life. So what is repentance and why is it vitally important?

The Greek word for repentance, *metanoia*, means 'a change of mind'. But a change of mind about what? About where life is found. Prior to coming to Christ our minds are shot through with the idea that life depends on such things as self-sufficiency, self-management, self-dependency, and so on. The Bible challenges this self-focused approach to living and says that in order for our lives to work the way God designed them, independence and self-reliance need to be marginal and not central. In other words, Jesus should be central. All humanity was created for a dependent relationship with God.

This is quite a radical thought for any mind to grapple with, but if there is no acceptance of it, no change of mind on this issue, the soul will not go on to experience a deep and developing relationship with God. No change of mind about where life is to be found – no spiritual progress. It is as simple as that.

FURTHER STUDY

Gal. 2:20;
Rom. 6:6;
Col. 2:1–20

1. What graphic way did Paul describe repentance?
2. What concern did Paul have for the Colossians?

Heavenly Father, help me examine my heart and decide just who is central in my life – You or me. Show me even more clearly how I can be more Christ-centred and less self-centred. In the name of Your Son I ask it. Amen.

God-dependent lives

FOR READING & MEDITATION – MATTHEW 4:12–25

*'From that time on Jesus began to preach,
"Repent, for the kingdom of heaven is near."' (v17)*

What strikes me as curious is that in many parts of the Church today, there doesn't seem to be any emphasis on repentance. Perhaps this arises from a misunderstanding of its implications and its call to respond. We are often very focused on action and less inclined to consider our inner attitudes, yet when I open my New Testament, what do I find? The theme appears repeatedly. Today's text tells us that Jesus' very first public message in His ministry was 'Repent'. We see from many other passages in the Gospels that He stresses this message again and again. Peter took up this same theme in the sermon he preached on the Day of Pentecost (see Acts 2:38). Indeed, the word 'repentance' appears in one form or another throughout the New Testament.

FURTHER STUDY

Isa. 55:7;
Acts 2:38;
1 John 1:9;
Luke 15:11–32

1. What has God promised to the penitent?

2. How did the prodigal son display repentance?

Why, then, is repentance often glossed over (generally speaking) in contemporary Christianity? Is it because in our anxiety to reach more people we avoid the seemingly thorny and arresting subject of repentance, and prefer the quicker sale of an easy prayer requiring minimal transformation? On one occasion I heard an evangelist tell his listeners: 'Pray this prayer after me, and you will have a mansion in heaven... perhaps even have charge of ten cities when Christ returns to this earth to establish His kingdom.' This really saddened me – it should be about Him, not us! If we are to live in the good of all that God wants for us, in the way He originally designed, we need to place Jesus at the centre. That means we are no longer living self-dependent lives but God-dependent lives. Happy are those who enter the Christian life with this clear understanding.

God, help me put first things first. I see that fruitful Christian living depends on You taking first place in my life. Help me search my soul. In Jesus' name. Amen.

CWR Ministry Events

PLEASE PRAY FOR THE TEAM

DATE	EVENT	PLACE	PRESENTER(S)
5 Jan	BA Counselling Year 1 resumes	Waverley Abbey House	Waverley Abbey College team
12 Jan	MA Therapeutic Counselling and Psychotherapy Years 1 and 2 resumes	WAH	Waverley Abbey College team
15 Jan	BA Counselling Year 4 resumes	Pilgrim Hall	Waverley Abbey College team
17 Jan	Overwhelmed: Finding Balance in a Fast-Paced World	WAH	Andy Peck
19 Jan	BA Counselling Year 2 resumes	PH	Waverley Abbey College team
20 Jan	Waverley Abbey College Open Day	PH	Pilgrim Hall team
22 Jan	BA Counselling Year 3 resumes	PH	Waverley Abbey College team
29 Jan	MA Counselling Year 2 resumes	WAH	Waverley Abbey College team
29 Jan – 2 Feb	January Bargain Break	PH	Pilgrim Hall team
25 Feb	Open the Roof regional event	Salvation Army, Folkestone, Kent	Andy Peck

Please pray for our students and tutors on our ongoing BA Counselling programme at Waverley Abbey College (which takes place at Waverley Abbey House and Pilgrim Hall), as well as our Certificate in Christian Counselling and MA Counselling qualifications.

We would also appreciate prayer for our ongoing ministry in Singapore and Cambodia, as well as the many regional events that will be happening around the UK this year.

For further information and a full list of CWR's courses, seminars and events, call **+44 1252 784719** or visit **www.cwr.org.uk/courses**

You can also download our free Prayer Track, which includes daily prayers, from **www.cwr.org.uk/prayertrack**

Flightless butterflies

FOR READING & MEDITATION – ACTS 26:1–20

'I preached that they should repent and...
prove their repentance by their deeds.' (v20)

During a conference, some evangelists asked me this question: 'Why don't we see more of the kind of new believers coming into today's Church that we used to get a few decades ago – those who from the very start seem "out and out" for Jesus?' I replied that I thought it had something to do with the way we present the truths of Christianity, and I told them the story I heard John White, a Christian psychiatrist, tell.

A butterfly, struggling to get out of its chrysalis, was given a helping hand by a well-meaning observer. As a result, however,

FURTHER STUDY

Luke 14:25–35;
Mark 10:28;
Luke 5:27–28

1. What was Jesus' message to the crowd who followed Him?

2. What was Peter able to say?

the butterfly was unable to fly, because it is in the struggle to emerge that it develops the strength to soar. The observer, intent on making it easy for the butterfly to leave the chrysalis, unintentionally contributed to its early demise.

We do something similar when we help people avoid the struggle that conscious, intentional repentance invariably brings. By trying to make things easier, we work not for them, but against them. The contemporary Church (with exceptions) is like an inexperienced carer, raising children with incomplete resources and knowledge – their health and growth is hampered by a lack of attention to basic principles. To return to the metaphor of the butterfly, in the Church today there are many butterflies unable to fly because when they emerged from their spiritual chrysalis, someone may have inadvertently struggled *for* them instead of *with* them. We can do this with misleading statements, incomplete truths or even by a misplaced emphasis. Increasingly, evangelism is finding ways to make it easy for people to be saved, but let's be careful that we do not make it easier than it should be.

Father God, stir us to put the emphasis where You put it – on the Lordship of Jesus and the need for us to put Him first in our lives from those very first steps in faith. In Christ's name we pray. Amen.

The beginning, not the end

FOR READING & MEDITATION – ACTS 2:29–41

*'Repent and be baptised, every one of you, in the name of Jesus
Christ for the forgiveness of your sins.' (v38)*

If repentance is such a crucial and important issue in our
pursuit of God, let's spend a few more days exploring what
the vast majority of people might say when asked about the
word 'repentance'. They will say that repentance is what is
required in order to become a Christian – that it is the way
into the Christian life. Now that is entirely true, but not true
entirely, because repentance is much more than that. One of
the first things written in Martin Luther's 95 Theses, which he
nailed to the door of the Castle Church in Wittenberg in 1517,
sparking off the Reformation, is this: 'When our Lord
and Master Jesus Christ said "Repent" He willed that
the entire life of the believer be one of repentance.'

**FURTHER
STUDY**

Mark 1:1–8;
Acts 3:17–26

1. How does
John prepare the
way for Jesus?

2. What,
according to
Peter, is the
outcome of
repentance?

What did Luther mean? As we said earlier, the
Greek word for repentance is *metanoia*, meaning a
change of mind. When we become a Christian, we
change our mind about running our life on our own
terms, deciding instead to surrender it to Jesus. That
is the initial act of repentance. Now this is where
many stop. They believe that they have made a
once-and-for-all decision. But is that initial act of
repentance the beginning and the end?

We read in the book of Revelation, that the church
in Ephesus had left their first love (Rev. 2:1–7). Jesus
said, in effect, 'You don't love me like you used to.' How were
they to recover their lost love for Jesus? We might have
suggested they start doing the things they hadn't been doing,
such as works of love or service. It is so easy to get involved in
works of reparation. But, as we shall see tomorrow, this wasn't
the way that Jesus, the wonderful counsellor, dealt with them.

**Father God, thank You that You have made a way for me to enter
into Your presence. May my life every day be one of repentance
and renewed thinking. In Jesus' name. Amen.**

Finding our way back

FOR READING & MEDITATION – REVELATION 2:1–7

*'Remember the height from which you have fallen!
Repent and do the things you did at first.' (v5)*

Today let's consider how Jesus, the wonderful counsellor, deals with the church at Ephesus. In today's text we find that He told the Ephesians to remember, repent, and then return to doing the things they did at first. And this is a wonderful pattern to follow. First, we seek to remember from where we have fallen. Then we repent and return to doing works of love. There needs to be the admission that we have moved away from Jesus and that we are now going to move back. That has to be a conscious decision. And it is the making of that conscious decision that is so often missing. Whenever we move away from our relationship with God, or whenever we find that something has come between Him and us, then the way back is through the door of repentance.

FURTHER STUDY

Ezek. 18:30–32;
Mark 1:14–20

1. How does Ezekiel exhort the people?

2. How do the disciples demonstrate their dependence on Christ?

Where do we find our life? It's so easy to echo Paul's words in Philippians 1:21 and say, 'For to me, to live is Christ'. But do we mean it? Often we forget what sin really is. Sin is pushing God out of the place He has reserved for Himself. We tend to think of sin as overt forms of behaviour, such as cheating, lying, stealing, swearing and rudeness. But sin is more often subtle than obvious. It's easy to move from dependency on Jesus to something else, and when we move away from dependence on Him, then in order to restore our relationship with Him we must repent.

This, I believe, is something so many forget on the journey of faith. Many believe repentance is a one-off act. But repentance is a change of mind about where life is found, and sometimes we seek life in something other than God. The entire life of the believer is to be one of repentance, as Martin Luther so rightly said.

Lord Jesus, please help me to remember how things once were and, if I have done so, to repent of relegating You and finding my life in something other than You. May I return to close relationship with You. Amen.

The first steps of repentance

FOR READING & MEDITATION – HOSEA 14:1–3

'Return... to the LORD your God. Your sins have been your downfall!'
(v1)

The verses we have read today are some of the most enlightening when it comes to this matter of repentance. As we have been saying, there is no way we can return to a right relationship with God without repentance. The teaching on repentance we find in Hosea helps us to move from independence to reliance upon God, and these verses show us a divine pattern we can follow.

'Return... to the LORD your God.' We have looked elsewhere for the energy to make our lives work; now we must transfer our dependence to God.

'Take words with you' (v2). When we come to God, we plan not to fall over our words. We take responsibility with a clear idea of what we are repenting of, and the clearer our understanding, the more profound our repentance. The prodigal son carefully rehearsed what he would say to his father when he returned home: 'I will set out and go back to my father and say to him: Father, I have sinned against heaven and against you. I am no longer worthy to be called your son' (Luke 15:18–19).

'Forgive all our sins' (v2). What is sin? It is 'me' in the place God reserved for Himself. We cannot rid ourselves of sin; it can only be forgiven.

'Receive us graciously, that we may offer the fruit of our lips' (v2). Repentance involves throwing ourselves on the mercy of God so that we may learn how to approach Him in true worship. The thought here is: 'Receive us so that we may rightly worship.' True worship flows from an understanding that the power to make our lives work is to be found in God through Christ – and nowhere else.

FURTHER STUDY

Psa. 51:1–6;
Lam. 3:22–26,
40–42;
2 Pet. 3:8–9

1. For what did David pray?

2. What words were to be used in the lament over sin?

Gracious Father, Your Word has such clarity and gives me all the directions I need for life. Help me to see the path I should take – and follow it. In Christ's name. Amen.

Further steps of repentance

FOR READING & MEDITATION – HOSEA 14:1–3

'Assyria cannot save us; we will not mount war-horses.' (v3)

We continue unpacking these verses from Hosea, which helpfully lay out principles that precede life-changing and life-saving repentance.

'Assyria cannot save us; we will not mount war-horses.' Assyria was a nation with horses and chariots, and so a pact with them looked like a sensible move. However, turning to Assyria would take Israel's dependence off of God – and in the end, Assyria was powerless. Do you perhaps have an 'Assyria' in your life?

FURTHER STUDY

Psa. 51:7–12;
Acts 17:25–31

1. What further steps of repentance did David take?

2. How did Paul confront idolatry in Athens?

'We will never again say "Our gods" to what our own hands have made' (v3). Only when we accept that the real issue underlying sin is idolatry (that is, choosing to devote ourselves to something other than the creator God) will we see how our self-sufficiency bypasses the divine scheme of things. Even our vain attempts to rely on our own strategies as we relate to others must be seen for what they are – idolatry.

'In you the fatherless find compassion' (v3). Fatherless children are unprotected children, defenceless and vulnerable to the point of helplessness. Repentance involves us accepting disappointments from which our souls would naturally shrink. The willingness to acknowledge our helplessness enables us to see how desperately we need God's love and mercy, and this causes us to turn to Him and become dependent upon Him. When we do, we find He is indeed a compassionate Father.

Repentance is the path that leads to life. It is not only the entrance into the Christian life, but also the means by which we make progress in our movement towards God.

Dear Father, I sincerely take these steps of repentance. I want to love with Your love, for then, and only then, can I kindle Your love in others. Amen.

Amazing!

FOR READING & MEDITATION – ROMANS 5:12–21

'how much more will those who receive God's abundant provision of grace… reign in life' (v17)

We have recognised over the past few days that one issue we must grasp if we are to go deeper with God is the need for a daily attitude of repentance. What is the next thing we will consider? It is how to avail ourselves of God's grace. Our text for today talks about 'those who receive God's abundant provision of grace'. Note particularly the word 'receive'. Though God's grace may be abundant, it only impacts our lives if it is received. But what do we mean by 'grace'? How can it be defined?

Grace is spoken of in both the Old and New Testaments, and the root meaning of the word is that of kindness and favour. In the New Testament it is used chiefly in connection with God's undeserved mercy in redeeming and restoring humankind. 'Grace', as undeserved favour, is a term still used in business – especially the world of insurance. A representative of a firm, for example, may write to a client and say something like this: 'In the circumstances you have no claim, but we will give you a certain sum as an act of grace.' They acknowledge no indebtedness, but out of their kindness (and in hope of business to come), they give the client something to which he has no legal right.

FURTHER STUDY

Acts 15:1–11;
Rom. 3:24;
Titus 3:7

1. What are some of the fruits of grace?

2. Write out your own definition of grace.

A definition of grace I like very much is this: 'Grace is the strength God gives us to obey His commands.' Grace is not just kindly platitudes, but an impartation of power too. We can be sure that the people who pass us on the road of discipleship and seem to know God in a much deeper way than we do have received more of that power, which God imparts 'unmerited and free'. It is by grace that they leap over all the barriers and diversions on their onward way. Grace truly is amazing!

Father, I cannot thank You enough for Your grace. I have no right to it, yet You bestow it freely. I praise Your name. Amen.

Always more to follow

FOR READING & MEDITATION – JAMES 4:1–17

'God opposes the proud but gives grace to the humble.' (v6)

We said yesterday that the people who travel past us on the road to knowing God, receive more of the grace that God pours out. The question inevitably arises in our minds: Why? Why have they received more grace? If, as we said, grace is undeserved favour, does that mean God has favourites? Is there something unpredictable about His allocation of help to His children?

Some secular writers have portrayed God as being like men and women, biased in His affections and having an inexplicable preference for one person and disinterest in another.

FURTHER STUDY

Rom. 5:1–15;
Titus 2:11;
1 Tim. 1:14

1. To whom did grace overflow?

2. What was Paul's testimony to Timothy?

But God does not take what we call 'a fancy' to some people and not others. While there is favour to be found in God, there is no favouritism. His favour moves to all who are willing and eager to receive it.

But to return to our question: Why do some receive more grace than others? I think the main reason is this – they know that there is grace to be had. Sometimes I come across Christians who think that God's only concern is to get us on to the pilgrim way, and that He then leaves us to our own devices.

You can identify such people by the way they talk about their conversion – and nothing more. They seem unconcerned about the truth that God's great goal is not simply to bring us into the Christian life, but to grow us in it. He is not content with calling us 'saints' but making us saints; not simply cancelling sin, but breaking its power over us. Those who receive God's grace are those who know He has plenty to give. Of this they are confident, and they keep it in mind all the time. When they have used what they have, they know there is always more to follow.

Father, however much I draw on Your grace, there is always more. I cannot draw heavily on many things but I can draw heavily on You. May this be more than an idea; may it be a fact. In Christ's name. Amen.

A throne of grace

FOR READING & MEDITATION – HEBREWS 4:1–16

*'Let us then approach the throne of grace with confidence,
so that we may... find grace' (v16)*

We are seeing that one reason why some Christians grow in faith more swiftly than others, and thus develop a closer relationship with God, is because they know how to draw on the resources of His grace. In their pursuit of God they open themselves to Him and He pours His grace out. Whenever I have talked with people who know God intimately, I have noticed that they view grace as a treasure above all treasures. It is not that they put no value on the things of earth, but they see grace as the most precious thing of all.

John Wesley, the founder of Methodism, had a friend called Fletcher of Madeley – a man who had travelled far in his relationship with God – who Wesley designated as his successor. He died before Wesley, however, and at his funeral Wesley took as his text Psalm 37:37: 'Mark the perfect man.' He told of how on one occasion, Fletcher had made a public utterance concerning the government of the day, which had greatly impressed its leaders. Soon after, the Lord Chancellor dispatched a representative to Fletcher's home to offer him some preferment or, as we would say, a promotion. The official was at some pains to hint delicately at his errand and said: 'The government would be very happy to... err... oblige in any way if... err... there was anything Mr Fletcher wanted...' 'How very kind,' was the great man's reply, 'but I want nothing... except more grace.'

That is the difference between those who know God deeply and those who don't. They look at the values of earth in the light of heaven and see that the only really valuable thing is – grace. 'Let me have that,' they say, 'and I am content.'

FURTHER STUDY

2 Cor. 8:9; 12:9;
2 Tim. 2:1–10

1. How did Paul describe grace at work?

2. What was Paul's admonition to Timothy?

**God, help me look at the values of earth in the light of heaven.
Show me the dangers of heaping together the treasures of earth.
May I come to recognise what has the highest value of all – Your
matchless grace. Amen.**

Effective service

FOR READING & MEDITATION – 1 CORINTHIANS 15:1–11

'I worked harder than all of them – yet not I,
but the grace of God that was with me.' (v10)

We considered yesterday the story of Fletcher of Madeley who, when approached by a government official and invited to name something he wanted, said: 'I want nothing... except more grace.' One wonders what account the official gave when he returned to the Lord Chancellor. 'He doesn't appear to want anything. Nothing we can offer seems to attract him. The only thing he wants is more grace!'

In his book, *The Pure in Heart* (now out of print), W.E. Sangster says that common to all who know God deeply is a high view of grace. They have learned to look at all the values of earth in the light of heaven. They have seen how it is ultimately illogical to put their trust in wealth, the meaninglessness of angling for applause, credits and titles, and they have come to the conclusion that the only really valuable thing in life is grace.

FURTHER STUDY

2 Cor. 1:1–12;
6:1;
1 Pet. 4:10

1. What was Paul's boast?

2. What did he urge the Corinthians?

Few will argue with the fact that the apostle Paul was one of the greatest Christians who has ever lived, and so it is interesting to note from today's passage that he laboured for God not in his own strength but in the strength God gave him. He makes clear that the key to fruitful Christian service is labouring not in the energy of one's own strength, but in the energy that comes from God. The grace of God is essential not only to live a holy life but to live a useful one also. The best way to serve others is to reach out to them in the strength that God gives to us. This is the point the great apostle is making. 'I worked harder... yet not I, but the grace of God that was with me.' The work of Jesus is best done by Jesus Himself, for no one else can do it. He who lives in us is best placed to strengthen and equip us to work with Him.

Holy God, help me to partner with You in Your work, rather than labouring in my own strength. I praise You that You are enough. Amen.

CWR

Pursuing God
...with books and resources

'*I did not want it to finish! I'm a mum of three young kids, and I managed to read it every day and spend time with God.*'
– Reader of *Transformed Life* by Dave Smith

Enabling you to dive deeper into the Bible, CWR's books and resources offer something for everyone. Through DVDs for small groups, books for children and young people, a whole range just for women and resources written especially for men, readers can explore how to apply the Bible to their daily lives, and pursue the God who loves them. Visit the website to discover more.

www.cwr.org.uk/resources

'A Christ not in us...'

FOR READING & MEDITATION – GALATIANS 2:11–21

*'I have been crucified with Christ and I no longer live,
but Christ lives in me.' (v20)*

It is noteworthy that throughout the ages, God's greatest servants have made clear that the impact they made was not a result of their own efforts, but the grace that God conveyed to them. We saw yesterday that the apostle Paul said his labours were energised by the grace given to him by God. He says something similar in today's reading: 'I no longer live... Christ lives in me.' The apostle had learned that it was not enough to give all of his strength to the work of the gospel, though he certainly did that; he had to receive Jesus' strength in order to do His work.

FURTHER STUDY

Eph. 3:1–9;
James 4:4–6;
1 Pet. 5:5

1. What did grace enable Paul to do?

2. What did James declare?

I have seen people suffer tremendously as a result of trying to live the Christian life in their own strength. We live dangerously when we try to do His work using natural energy alone. On one occasion, I was present at a dinner given in honour of a certain bishop. During the after-dinner speeches, I heard a layman make a terrible blunder when he declared: 'Bishop, we are both doing God's work; you in your way, and I in His.' Let's pause and ask ourselves: Is that me? Am I doing God's work in my own way or in His?

'A Christ not in us, imparting His grace to us,' said the great preacher William Law, 'is the same as a Christ not ours.' I don't know about you but I find those words incredibly challenging. Is this why so many of us never quite go as deeply with God as we could? We have received Jesus but we do not allow Him to diffuse Himself through all our being, to animate us with His life and Spirit. Let William Law's words strike deep into your soul: 'A Christ not in us, imparting His grace... is the same as a Christ not ours.'

Gracious and loving Father, may I do things Your way, not my way. Give me the wisdom, I pray, to know the difference. Amen.

Grace upon grace

FOR READING & MEDITATION – JOHN 1:1–17

'From the fulness of his grace we have all received one blessing after another.' (v16)

Although I like the New International Version, I often like to see how other translations have phrased certain passages. For example, the Amplified Bible translates today's passage like this: 'For out of His fullness (abundance) have we all received [all had a share and we were all supplied with] one grace after another *and* spiritual blessing upon spiritual blessing, *and* even favor upon favor *and* gift [heaped] upon gift.' I love the phrase 'one grace after another'. The thought contained in the original text is of grace succeeding grace.

Our capacity to receive grace at any level depends on our use of it at the lowest level. Refuse God's grace at one level of your life and you make it difficult to receive it at another level. We are to use the present proffered grace to be granted the grace that succeeds it. One preacher describes it this way: 'I remember when I sat for my first scholarship. I recall going to my professor and saying: "What will I do when I have used the paper up?" He laughed. "You needn't worry about that," he said. "When you have used all you have, just ask for more." Much relieved I added: "Will he give me all I want?" "No," replied the professor, "but he will give you all you can use."'

God is eager to give His grace to every one of us, and there is so much of it. As an old hymn puts it: 'Grace is flowing like a river, millions there have been supplied'.

Like manna for the children of Israel, you can have all you are able to use, but it's fresh daily. How good are you at receiving God's grace? Not talking about it, receiving it?

FURTHER STUDY

Phil. 4:14–19; Eph. 1:7; 2:7

1. What was Paul confident of?

2. How did he describe God's grace?

My Father and my God, show me how to receive Your grace – really receive it. Help me to throw myself on You, to be less self-reliant and more God-reliant. Help me understand this even more, dear Lord. Please help me. In Jesus' name. Amen.

Moving off the sandbank

FOR READING & MEDITATION – GALATIANS 5:1–15

'You were running a good race. Who cut in on you and kept you from obeying the truth?' (v7)

As you read the words of our text today do you not sense the disappointment the apostle Paul felt over some of the Galatians? 'You were running a good race.' You were! Ah, there's the problem. They started well but they had been sidetracked.

Might Paul say as much to you and me? We were keen once. It wasn't just our youth. We were responding to grace. It came in like the waves of the sea – grace succeeding grace – and we allowed ourselves to be carried along by it. Then the time came when God led us to some new task or challenge and maybe surrender – of time, money, talents – and we veered away. God never presents us with a task without extending the grace to enable us to do it. When we refused the task, we also refused the grace. That's when we ran onto the sandbank. People who started after us swept past us, not because they are specially favoured, but because they opened themselves to the grace God provides. Age or illness may limit us, but they don't need to stop us from pursuing God.

FURTHER STUDY

Phil. 3:7–16;
1 Tim. 4:15;
1 Cor. 9:24

1. What was Paul able to say?

2. What were Paul's words to Timothy?

Here's what I suggest. Before you go to sleep tonight, get alone and be quiet with God. Review your life in God's light. Ask yourself: Where did I fall out of the race? Was it here... or here... or here...? Invite God to show you the place where you drew back. When He does, ask for forgiveness of your unwillingness to use His grace (there will be grace available for you to face up to this) and tell Him you want to be back in the race again, keeping pace, pursuing God, and going forward with the most passionate souls you know. It will delight God and make the angels sing. 'Look,' they will say, 'he (or she) is moving again. Hallelujah!'

Lord God, may this day be a turning point in my spiritual journey. Help me take this truth to heart that when I refuse Your challenge I refuse the grace that goes along with it. Today I move off the sandbank by grace. Amen.

Two extremes

FOR READING & MEDITATION – PSALM 68:11–20

*'Praise be to the Lord, to God our Saviour,
who daily bears our burdens.' (v19)*

W e continue identifying various elements that become our
spiritual priorities if we are to pursue a more intimate
relationship with God. The next principle to explore – if we
are to go deeper with God – is to spend time with Him. This
means taking time to regularly read His Word, talk to Him in
prayer, and cultivate the spiritual sensitivity to listen for His
voice speaking directly to our souls.

It is a great tragedy when spiritual leaders forget to
emphasise the need for us all to regularly spend time with God
in prayer and reading His Word. This de-emphasis
is, in my opinion, due to many things, but two in
particular. First, it is a reaction to the legalism of
past days. At one time, most Christians were told
that the life of discipleship turned on whether or
not you established a daily quiet time, and you must
never waver from it. In my youth I heard one Bible
teacher say: 'If you don't begin every day by reading a
chapter of the Bible and spending at least 30 minutes
in prayer, then you have no right to go into the day
expecting God to bless it.'

**FURTHER
STUDY**

Psa. 119:1–15,
72,97;
Jer. 23:29

1. What did the
psalmist say he
would not do?

2. What did
Jeremiah liken
God's Word to?

But I don't believe this is true. There are many
reasons why it might not be possible to begin every day with
a quiet time. God wants to meet with us and bless us, whatever
our morning routine.

However, in turning from the legalism of the past, many
have replaced it with a more casual approach to personal
devotions. If they don't feel like it, they don't find a time to be
with God. And that, I suggest, is as risky as the legalism from
which they might have turned away.

**Lord, help me make it the habit of a lifetime to spend time each
day with You. Remind me to make this a priority, Father. Amen.**

Two customs

FOR READING & MEDITATION – LUKE 4:14–30

'on the Sabbath day he went into the synagogue, as was his custom.'
(v16)

We said yesterday that one reason why there is a more casual approach (generally speaking) to personal devotions in the Christian Church today than there was some time ago is that it is a reaction to the legalism of past days. The other reason (so I believe) is when we assume that a quiet time is not at all necessary.

In the early days of the Charismatic renewal, many of its leaders from the historic denominations who had been fed on a diet of legalism began to emphasise (quite rightly) the joy of knowing Jesus' presence through the indwelling Spirit every hour of the day. I often used to hear people say in Charismatic services: 'Now I don't have to have a daily quiet time in order to feel God's presence; I can feel it every hour of the day. Every waking minute is a quiet time.' While true, this thinking is also dangerous. The danger lies not in emphasising that we are in God's presence every hour of the day, but the de-emphasis on finding sacred spaces in a secular society for spending time alone with Him in personal prayer and reading His Word. In fairness, most leaders of the Charismatic renewal did not teach or encourage people to forget their personal times of devotion, but many came to believe they could get through the day simply by speaking in tongues.

FURTHER STUDY

Matt. 6:5–15;
14:23;
Luke 5:16

1. What did Jesus teach about prayer?

2. How did He demonstrate it?

Nothing will or can be a substitute for the private and personal time we spend in prayer and communion with God. Jesus knew and sensed the presence of God with Him and in Him to a degree we will probably never fully experience here on this earth, but it is said of Him in Scripture that He had two 'customs'. One custom was to go regularly to the house of God; the other was to pray regularly. I think that says it all.

Lord Jesus, if You needed to spend time alone with Your Father in personal prayer, then how much more do I need to also. Help me steer a middle path between legalism and casualness. For Your own dear name's sake. Amen.

Plan and passion

FOR READING & MEDITATION – PSALM 34:1–22

'*I sought the LORD, and he answered me*' (v4)

When people came up to me at seminars or conferences and asked: 'How can I develop a better relationship with God?' I invariably replied: 'Spend time with Him.' The more time we spend with our families and friends, the better we get to know them. It is the same with God too.

People often asked me to give them a plan on how to have a quiet time. Here is one I used to give people many years ago. Decide on the amount of time you can spend, preferably in the morning. (The morning is best because it tunes your soul for the day. Having fixed the time, stick to it.) Take your Bible and a notebook and read a passage carefully. Let it soak in. Make a note of anything that comes to you. Follow this with prayer, mentioning any requests or personal petitions you may have. Finally, relax and listen expectantly to see if God has something to say to you. It is far easier to talk than listen, so don't worry if for some weeks or months nothing comes. Tuning in to God takes time and practice.

However, later I was reluctant to give people that plan without highlighting the pitfall of depending on a structure rather than on the direction of the Holy Spirit. I imagine most of us would prefer to spend time with God with a plan than to abandon ourselves to the Holy Spirit and wait upon Him. A structure can be both useful and helpful, but as we learn to be alone with God we can, on occasions, simply enjoy His company and presence without even saying a word. Time with God becomes more alive when we approach it with passion instead of a plan. Good marriages thrive on spontaneity, special intentional occasions and passion. So does a relationship with the Lord.

FURTHER STUDY

Psa. 46:1–11;
Isa. 30:15;
32:17

1. When can we know God?

2. Find some time today to be still in His presence.

Father, help me come to my times with You with expectancy – expectancy that my weakness shall become strength, my doubt become faith, and my passion become stronger. In Jesus' name. Amen.

A Father and a friend

FOR READING & MEDITATION – LUKE 11:1–13

'Ask and it will be given to you; seek and you will find' (v9)

The more I write about the need for a daily or an intentional time with God, the more uncomfortable I feel. I asked myself why this should be, and this is what I came to.

The great danger of a quiet time is that we will use it as an opportunity to petition God rather than to get to know Him and be known by Him. I thought back to something I remember reading a while ago, where the writer said that the older he got, the less involved he became in petitionary prayer. 'The strange thing is,' said the writer (and I am paraphrasing), 'the more I pray for things the less my prayers seem to get answered. I think God is leading me on to ask less and less for things and more and more for Him.' Then he expressed this profound thought: 'Prayer is taking part in the process of being known.'

FURTHER STUDY

Job 37:14–24;
Psa. 4:4; 131:2

1. What was Elihu's admonition to Job?

2. What was the psalmist able to say?

I glanced up as I wrote those words and looked out at the trees in my garden. God knows everything there is to know about those trees, but because they are trees and not people they cannot join in the process of being known. God knows all there is to know about me, of course, but that objective knowledge is quite different from the process of drawing close to Him in prayer and letting Him know me through my opening up to Him. One is objective knowledge, the other experiential. And what is breathtakingly awe-inspiring about all this is that in every spiritual tête-à-tête I hold with God, He seeks to draw my soul into such a relationship with Him that I know Him not simply as someone who answers prayer, but as a Father and a friend. Such knowledge is almost too good to be true. But it is also too good not to be true!

My Father and my friend, may my times of communion with You be more than just a petitioner talking to a supplier. Help me open myself fully to You. In Jesus' name I ask it. Amen.

Knowing God

FOR READING & MEDITATION – PHILIPPIANS 3:1–11

'I want to know Christ and the power of his resurrection' (v10)

We talked yesterday of prayer as part of the process of being known. We know people or are known by people to the degree that we spend time with them. This is the simple but profound truth we are exploring. We cannot have a deep and ongoing relationship with God unless we are prepared to spend time with Him.

It is not my purpose at this moment to explore the philosophy of prayer, but I do feel it will be helpful to some if I elaborate a little on how God delights also to be known. The Father is known by the other members of the Trinity (and they by Him), and that undoubtedly brings Him great pleasure. But He longs also to be known by His children. There is something in the heart of God that enjoys being known. He is a relational being. The account of Abraham's pleading with God for his nephew Lot (Gen. 18:23–33) illustrates beautifully the two-way relationship that Abraham enjoyed with His God. In the Authorised Version, in Genesis 18:19, the Lord says of Abraham: 'For I know him…' It seems that the Lord had such a confidence in Abraham that He was prepared to reveal to him what He was going to do to Sodom (v17). But Abraham too knew the character of His God that he respectfully yet audaciously pleaded his case that Sodom might be spared if there were ten righteous people in it. Although God is not dependent on His creation, in some mystical way we enrich the heart of God by knowing Him. I am not saying that by knowing God we add to Him or complete Him. That would be untrue. But we can, by our deeper knowledge of Him, bring Him pleasure. And what better reason for knowing God is there?

FURTHER STUDY

John 17:1–5;
Jer. 9:23–24;
Job 19:25

1. What is the essence of eternal life?

2. What should our boast be?

Heavenly Father, I am grateful for the way in which I have come to know You, but I long to know You still more. In Christ's name I pray. Amen.

Unstated times

'But when you pray, go into your room, close the door and pray to your Father, who is unseen.' (v6)

Today we continue to explore the truth that in order to go deeper with God we need to spend quality time with Him. How amazing to be invited to sit quietly in His presence, talk with Him, and let Him talk with us! Those who say they can develop their relationship with God without intentional times of prayer and the reading of His Word are misleading themselves. Jesus (as we saw) is our best example. He knew God's presence better than anyone, yet He made time to be alone with His Father and talk to Him in private prayer.

FURTHER STUDY

Acts 10:1–9,30;
James 5:17

1. What was the pattern of Peter and Cornelius?

2. How focused was Elijah?

To say that we can develop a rich relationship with God by recognising His presence but not taking time to have a spiritual focus, is as a bit like expecting to stay physically healthy without having regular meals. During my travels, I often asked Christians I met if they had a daily or regular quiet time, and sometimes the answers I received surprised me. One man told me: 'Yes, I get up early, sit quietly in my garden and watch the birds feeding or the goldfish swimming in the pond... and I feel rejuvenated in my spirit and ready to start the day.' Is this really a time spent with God?

The whole purpose of the quiet time is to take in the spiritual resources of God. Nature is wonderful and restorative, but for the intake of spiritual resources we need the blessing that comes not from nature but from the Word of God and prayer. God offers us infinite resources for the asking – and taking. The quiet time is where the soul grows receptive and where prayer becomes powerful. As a result, we gain the quiet heart that in turn becomes quiet confidence, and that becomes quiet power.

Father God, deepen my desire to meet with You daily. Help me make my meeting times with You one of life's great priorities. In Jesus' name. Amen.

CWR

Pursuing God
...with daily Bible reading

'*I am amazed and so encouraged by this
month's notes. I feel like they were written
just for me. I have heard God speak
through them in incredible ways.*'
– Reader of *Inspiring Women Every Day*

Getting into God's Word daily, and practically
applying it to life, helps us live in step with God's
plans. With eight different Bible reading notes for
adults, teenagers and children to choose from
– all of which include Bible readings, reflections
and prayers – we can enhance our own daily walk
with God or encourage someone else with a gift
subscription. Visit the website to discover more.

www.cwr.org.uk/biblenotes

Ah, what then?

FOR READING & MEDITATION – PSALM 46:1–11

'Be still, and know that I am God' (v10)

We spend one more day reflecting on the need for a daily or regular intentional time with God if we are to know Him better. Though we are continually in God's presence, it is necessary also to have regular times when we focus on Him and on His Word, the Bible.

In these times the soul is stilled so that it concentrates on God, and it is through this concentration that the spiritual life is deepened. Christian Blaise Pascal once declared that 'Nearly all the ills of life spring from this simple source, that we are unable to sit still for long in a quiet room.' Contemporary culture seems to find it difficult to sit quietly for long. There is far too much going on to distract us; there is always something else going on that breaks the stillness.

FURTHER STUDY

Psa. 33:17–22; 62:1–2; 130:5–6; 40:1

1. What did the psalmist do?

2. What was the result?

Sitting still can be therapeutic, but imagine if in the stillness we meet with God? We then receive spiritual therapy. God waits to offer us infinite resources – for the asking and the taking. The quiet time is where the soul grows receptive, where prayer becomes a place of healing – an oasis of peace, where the touch of His presence becomes as real and as dramatic as the touch of the woman on the hem of Jesus' garment, where peace flows into our turbulence, where love resolves our resentments, where joy heals our griefs, and where we enter into the process of being known. The quiet time shuts us in with God, the door closes upon us, and then infinite resources flood into our soul. The door opens and we move out, with an increased awareness of God, ready to face a world that knows so little about Him. There is, as we have said, great benefit in stillness, but when we meet with God in the stillness – ah, what then?

My Father and my God, I long to meet with You in the stillness. Help me to make space for silence, and protect me from distractions, I pray. In Jesus' name. Amen.

Can God be trusted?

FOR READING & MEDITATION – PSALM 20:1–9

'Some trust in chariots and some in horses, but we trust in the name of the LORD our God.' (v7)

We consider now another important aspect of pursuing a deeper relationship with God – confidence in His character. Is God good, and can He be trusted? The manner in which we answer this question is, again, crucial to our ongoing relationship with Him. If we have doubts about His character – His justice, for example – it will most certainly affect the way we view Him and approach Him.

You may have heard the story of the farmer whose one and only tractor failed. So he decided to walk across the fields to a neighbouring farmer, who he knew had three. As he strode to the neighbour's farmhouse, he reflected on what he had heard others say about this farmer. On one occasion, he had heard that he refused to contribute to a fund for a villager who'd been in a serious accident. He also remembered that he never appeared at any of the village's social events, and he had heard somewhere that he had a reputation as a skinflint. More negative thoughts about the farmer entered his head, and by this time he found himself at the door of the farmhouse. The farmer, who had seen him coming across the fields, appeared at the doorway and asked: 'What's the problem?' 'I've come to tell you,' said the man, 'that you can keep your miserable old tractor!'

Many do not realise how profoundly the way we think about God and His character influences the way we worship Him, the way we work for Him and the way we witness for Him. Doubts about the goodness of God (even subconsciously) will result in our souls keeping their distance from Him. If we do not have confidence in Him, we will not desire a close relationship with Him.

FURTHER STUDY

Neh. 9:19–25;
Psa. 23:6

1. What did the children of Israel revel in?

2. What was the psalmist's conviction about his life?

Father, help me deal with any doubts that I might have about Your goodness. Show me Your character, Lord. I trust in You. Amen.

Doubt and disobedience

FOR READING & MEDITATION – GENESIS 3:1–19

'He said to the woman, "Did God really say, 'You must not eat from any tree in the garden'?"' (v1)

We continue exploring the truth that unless we have a strong conviction that God is entirely trustworthy and perfect in character, we will not desire a deep and ongoing relationship with Him. Yesterday we spoke of the distance from God our souls might experience when we entertain doubts about His goodness. Do you realise that the reason for the distance between God and the first human couple in the Garden of Eden was doubt about God's goodness? Doubt about God soon leads to dislike of God, and dislike of God soon leads to disobedience.

FURTHER STUDY

Psa. 145:1–13; 31:19; 16:2

1. What do the people of God celebrate?

2. What did the psalmist say to the Lord?

When Eve responded to the serpent's insinuation that God did not have her best interests at heart (by withholding something from her), the doubt she entertained soon led to dislike of God, and then it was relatively easy to take the next step and disobey Him. The moment her doubt about God's goodness expressed itself in taking the forbidden fruit, the foundation on which her relationship with God was established – trust – crumbled beneath her feet. Adam rapidly followed her in committing the same kind of sin (doubt about God's goodness) and then, inevitably, distance replaced closeness.

Since the Fall, everyone born into this world has within their nature a basic distrust of God. Paul puts it like this: 'the sinful mind is hostile to God' (Rom. 8:7). The word 'hostility' can be translated 'enmity'. No one trusts someone they regard as an enemy. Distance between humankind and God arose when the first human couple doubted His goodness. Closeness between human beings and God comes when we have confidence in His goodness. As we said yesterday, no confidence – no real relationship.

God my Father, help me have an unshakable confidence in Your character so that there is no room for doubt. I want no distance between us, but an ever-growing closeness. Grant it, in Jesus' name. Amen.

Close the distance

FOR READING & MEDITATION – MATTHEW 7:15–29

'everyone who... does not put [Jesus' words] into practice is like
a foolish man who built his house on sand.' (v26)

'The biggest problem we face in the Christian life,' said Dr Cynddylan Jones, a famous Welsh preacher, 'is distance.' He continued: 'The only way that distance can be overcome is by having the perspective of Job who said: "Though He slay me, yet will I hope in Him."'

When I talked with counsellors in training to try to identify underlying causes to problems, I would explore with them that what they are listening for as a counsellee tells his or her story is distance. That's what I believe underlies many problems that bring people into counselling. This does not mean we ignore or make light of the surface and presenting problems with which people may be struggling. But the plain fact is this – when we are close to God and have a deep and intimate relationship with Him, we may feel downcast but not destroyed. Therefore, every Christian counsellor's ultimate goal is to help to close any distance there may be between the person and God, and to develop spiritual oneness. Counselling is not effective or complete until this is accomplished.

How does distance come between us and God? There are many reasons – bitterness and resentment against another, persistent sin, the lack of a regular time spent in God's presence – but mostly it arises through a lack of trust. If you cut your way through the maze of human troubles that's what you find – an inability to trust. That's what happened in the Garden of Eden, and that's what happens in our personal Garden of Eden also. To try to develop a close relationship with God and fail to deal with this most basic issue is about as effective as building a skyscraper on an acre of sand.

FURTHER STUDY

James 4:7–11;
Prov. 3:5–6;
29:25;
Heb. 10:22

1. When does God come near to us?

2. How should we draw near to God?

Father God, although there are many things that bring about distance between You and me, the most basic is lack of trust. Help me settle this issue once and for all over the next few days. In Christ's name I pray. Amen.

Where is God?

FOR READING & MEDITATION – PSALM 74:1–23

'Rise up, O God, and defend your cause; remember how fools mock you all day long.' (v22)

How do we develop trust in the goodness of God when so much that is happening in the world seems to contradict it? Men, women and children are suffering and dying in their thousands around the world, yet, if God is good, why does He allow such things?

Dr M. Scott Peck, in his book *The Road Less Travelled*, opens with these words: 'Life is difficult. This is a great truth because once we truly see this truth, we transcend it.' I have great difficulty with some of Dr Scott Peck's statements but I fully endorse these remarks. Once we accept the fact that life is difficult – that the mystery of why disasters and suffering occur will never be fully solved while we are here on earth – then we will stop demanding that a satisfactory answer be found and begin to get on with life.

FURTHER STUDY

Psa. 73:1–17; 25:8; 34:8

1. What was the psalmist's conclusion about God?

2. What did he struggle with?

Christians, I have found, go down different routes regarding this matter of suffering. One is to close their eyes and pretend that seemingly overwhelming problems are not there. But as I have said before, integrity requires that we face whatever is true. The grim reality of why a good and sovereign God allows suffering in His world is beyond the scope of these devotional meditations. However, let's not blind our eyes to these facts and pretend they are untrue just because at first sight they appear to contradict the concept of God's goodness. Pretence can never be our refuge. Let's be willing to look at these things, unpleasant and terrible though they be, and allow ourselves to be moved by them. When we face life honestly and allow ourselves to be shaken by what we see, then, and only then, are we ready for God to speak.

Gracious and loving heavenly Father, give me the courage not to bury my head in the sand and pretend there are no problems. Help me stand even when I cannot understand. For Your own dear name's sake. Amen.

CWR

Pursuing God
...through counselling

'I've been equipped to be more aware of certain areas that may be affecting a person's thinking, behaviour, choices and growth, and to help them on the path to wholeness in Christ.'
– Introduction to Biblical Care and Counselling course delegate

For over thirty years, CWR has been developing and offering counselling training that is underpinned by a Christian world-view. Now established as Waverley Abbey College, our training ranges from introductory courses to university validated programmes. Many of our students progress to become practising counsellors, and you can locate and contact them using our Find a Counsellor directory. Visit the website to discover more.

www.cwr.org.uk/counselling

The God who is there

FOR READING & MEDITATION – JOB 42:1–17

'My ears had heard of you but now my eyes have seen you.' (v5)

We ended yesterday with what you might have thought was a puzzling sentence: 'When we face life honestly and allow ourselves to be shaken by what we see, then and only then, are we ready for God to speak.' Let me expand.

The book of Job, as you know, records the story of a godly man who underwent some of the most bitter experiences imaginable. At first, Job says very little about his difficulties, but later in the book he begins to face the reality of what has happened to him and declares that if he could have an interview with God, he would tell Him exactly what he thought of Him (Job 23:1–17). It was when he faced his hardships, recognised how he really felt and admitted it, that God came to him and answered him (Job 38:1–41:34). We need never be afraid of admitting that what we see around us doesn't match up with what we know about the character of God. To blind our eyes to the realities of life for fear that what we observe might turn us against God is deception and distraction. We can face difficult issues, for it is when we do so that we are ready to hear God speak. When we refuse to face reality, then the spiritual antennae of our souls are dampened from hearing His voice. We fear that we might hear something to make us even more uncertain of God, and thus prefer to take refuge in illusion.

When Job faced the reality of his situation and how he really felt, then he was ready for God to speak. But notice God didn't give any answers to Job's questions. He gave Himself. Job had an encounter with God that more than satisfied him. He could live without answers when he knew that God was there.

FURTHER STUDY

Isa. 40:1–31;
Psa. 89:6;
1 Chron. 17:20

1. What question did Isaiah ask?

2. How did he answer it?

Loving Father, the more I learn about You the more wonderful I see You are. Help me to bring all my doubts and fears directly to You. Do for me what You did for Job – enrich me with Your presence. In Jesus' name. Amen.

Accepting the inevitable

FOR READING & MEDITATION – JOB 36:1–15

'But those who suffer he delivers in their suffering; he speaks to them in their affliction.' (v15)

Regular readers will recall that I often refer to Oswald Chambers' statement that 'Life is more tragic than orderly.' Chambers knew that unless we are willing to grapple with this truth and accept it, we will be plagued by inner *oughts* and *shoulds* that lead us down the road of illusion. We can find ourselves saying 'It ought not to be like this' or 'Things should be different' – and sadly the only thing this kind of demandingness produces is frustration and anger.

The Fall has turned this fair universe of God's into a shambles, and though much about the world is still beautiful, accidents, disasters, and suffering prevail. And these will continue until the time when God brings all things to a conclusion. There is nothing wrong with wishing that things were not so, but when we demand that they be different – when we say the effects of the Fall must be reversed and reversed now – we will find ourselves feeling fed up and frustrated.

Life is difficult, and though God, through prayer, does intervene miraculously in some situations, life will go on being more 'tragic than orderly' until Jesus returns and finalises His plans for this fallen world. This is reality – and the sooner we face it, the better. True faith is not built upon illusion but upon reality. We may not like things the way they are in this world, but to avoid facing them because they don't match up with what we know about God only shows that we need to understand God's ways better. As I have been stressing, it is only when we face honestly the harsh realities of life that we become ready for God to speak to us.

FURTHER STUDY

Heb. 11:1–40;
2 Cor. 11:16–29;
4:7–10

1. What is faith?
2. List some of the difficult circumstances of life faced in the light of faith.

Lord God, when there is no answer to hard questions, I ask You to step in and give me not an answer but Yourself. I can live without answers, but I cannot live without You. Stay close to me my Father. In Jesus' name. Amen.

Messed up theology

FOR READING & MEDITATION – JOB 13:1–15

'Though he slay me, yet will I hope in him' (v15)

A friend of mine, who is a lecturer and practitioner in the field of Christian counselling, says that one of the things he likes to do with his students is to challenge their theology. He does so by asking them difficult questions about the realities of the universe in order to see how they attempt to square these issues with their view of God. 'God always answers the prayer of faith,' said one of his students. 'Then why,' he asked the student, 'did I pray for an hour for my father who was desperately sick to have a good night, and then hear that he had the worst night since he had been in hospital?' 'You didn't pray in faith,' replied the student.

FURTHER STUDY

Dan. 3:13–30;
Hab. 3:16–18;
Psa. 46:2

1. How did the Hebrew youths demonstrate faith in God?

2. What does Habakkuk declare?

That's the kind of glib answer many people would give to that question. But it isn't as easy as that. When my wife was dying with cancer, people made similar statements to me. Such people can't sit quietly in the presence of mystery and say: 'I don't understand why this is so, but nevertheless I still believe God is good.' They must have some kind of answer that they can hold on to because when they have no answers they have no faith. Faith is Job saying: 'Though he slay me, yet will I hope in him.'

Anyone can believe when there are explanations and answers. The person who goes on to know God in a deep and intimate way is the one who can affirm that God is good even though there may be a thousand appearances to the contrary. We may be very conscious that we have not yet arrived at that place of absolute trust in God. Nevertheless, we are making progress when there is a deep longing within that we might come to the place of trusting God even when we cannot trace Him.

God, bring me closer day by day to that place of deep confidence and absolute trust. May I know You so deeply that nothing I see around me will shake or shatter my belief in Your unchanging goodness. Amen.

The old rugged cross

FOR READING & MEDITATION – ROMANS 5:1–11

*'But God demonstrates his own love for us in this:
While we were still sinners, Christ died for us.' (v8)*

We spend one last day reflecting on the fact that to develop a deep and intimate relationship with God it is essential to learn to have confidence in His character. Can we believe that God is good, even though things may be happening around us that seemingly contradict that fact? One place we can go when we are assailed by doubts about God's goodness is the cross. At Calvary we are given undeniable evidence that God is good. We can come to the cross when in doubt, and remind ourselves that a God who would give His only Son to die for us simply has to be all-goodness. A songwriter put it like this:

God is love, I see it in the earth around me;
God is love, I feel it in the sky above me;
God is love, all nature doth agree;
But the greatest proof of His love to me... is Calvary.

FURTHER STUDY

Gal. 6:1–14;
1 Cor. 1:17;
Eph. 2:16;
Col. 1:20

1. How did Paul view the cross?

2. Spend some time contemplating the cross today.

Many things about the cross are mysterious, but there is no mystery about divine goodness. At Calvary it shines out for all to see. I often wonder to myself what was happening that was good when my wife was dying of cancer. I couldn't see anything, but because I know God is good, I accepted that something good was being worked out. A good God was in charge, and I am prepared to wait for the clarification of that until I get to heaven. Then I know He will tell me Himself.

God is good, no matter what the appearances to the contrary. The 'old rugged cross' makes that crystal clear. Let us hold to it, come what may. It is here that our debts were settled once and for all. Yours, mine and all who call upon His restorative and redemptive name.

Lord, I am so thankful for the cross. It is the one place in a dark and mysterious universe where light breaks through. Help me interpret the darkness by the light, not the light by the darkness. In Jesus' name. Amen.

The stamp of eternity

FOR READING & MEDITATION – ISAIAH 6:1–13

'"Whom shall I send? And who will go for us?"...
I said, "Here am I. Send me!"' (v8)

Another issue to consider as we pursue the question of how we can go deeper with God is that of worship. There is little doubt that those who know God intimately are those who know how to worship Him. The Shorter Westminster Catechism asks the question, 'What is the chief end of man?' and answers it in this way: 'The chief end of man is to glorify God and enjoy Him for ever.'

Our primary task in this world is not to be workers, but worshippers. A.W. Tozer, who suggested that worship was the missing jewel of the Evangelical Church, put it like this: 'We're here to be worshippers first and workers second. We take a convert and immediately make a worker out of him. God never meant it to be so. God meant that a convert should learn to be a worshipper and after that learn to be a worker. The work done by a worshipper will have eternity in it.' Powerful words. Those who wish to go deeper with God will give themselves more to the worship of God than they do to the work of God. Indeed, it should count as a warning to us when we become more preoccupied with working for God than worshipping God.

FURTHER STUDY

Psa. 95:6;
John 4:1–26;
1 Chron. 16:29

1. What does the psalmist encourage us to do?

2. How are we to worship?

We need have no concern that we give ourselves too much to worship and consequently neglect our work for God, because no one can worship God without the necessity of service and action being impressed upon him or her. A vision of God, such as Isaiah saw in the Temple, leads inevitably to the call to serve. 'Who will go for us?' is the cry of the Trinity. The worshipper will contentedly respond: 'Here am I, send me.' And the work done by a worshipper will, as Tozer says so effectively, have the stamp of eternity upon it.

Lord, help me, I pray, to be a worshipper first and a worker second. Let all I do for You flow out of my worship of You so that my service will have the mark of eternity upon it. In Jesus' name. Amen.

CWR

Pursuing God

...in your church and small group

'*Even though we were looking at a familiar book of the Bible, my group found the guide the most helpful, inspirational and challenging study book we've ever used. I've recommended it to our whole church!*'
– Reader of a *Cover to Cover* Bible study guide

We are passionate about equipping the whole Church and small groups to be effective in their ministry and time spent together. We have a wide range of resources to inspire and equip those leading a church or organising and planning small groups. Visit the website to discover more.

www.cwr.org.uk/fyc

The one thing needed

FOR READING & MEDITATION – LUKE 10:38–42

'but only one thing is needed.' (v42)

We said yesterday that God wants us to be worshippers first and workers second, and nowhere is this truth more clearly illustrated than in the passage before us today.

Martha, bustling about in her kitchen, is frustrated because her sister Mary is listening at the feet of Jesus, rather than helping to get things done. Jesus, with characteristic insight, draws a line between the urgent and the important when He says: 'There is really only one thing worth being concerned about. Mary has discovered it – and I won't take it away from her!' (v42, TLB). Martha's concern to be hospitable was not being ignored by Jesus; He was simply highlighting that when it comes to priorities worship comes first, work second. Interestingly, the Great Commission was given to worshipping people. Matthew writes: 'When they saw [Jesus], they worshipped him... Then Jesus... said, "... go and make disciples of all nations"' (Matt. 28:17–19).

How true it is that unless we are involved with Jesus Christ in a loving and worshipping relationship, we have nothing of eternal value to offer to a needy world. Let's draw a line and reach a definite conclusion about this before moving any further – our worship of God takes priority over our work for God. When this happens, then we will get the right balance of work we are to do with Him. It is not Jesus who loads us with tasks that bend and break us. These come from our compulsions rather than from Christ. In the atmosphere of worship we see more clearly what we can do, and our work becomes a daily joy instead of a daily grind (see the principle of worship before tasks we fulfil in Romans 12).

FURTHER STUDY

Exod. 20:1–21;
Psa. 29:2; 99:5

1. What importance does the Lord place on worship?

2. What is the admonition of the psalmist?

Gracious and loving heavenly Father, help me perceive that 'only one thing is needed' for life's priorities to fall into place – the worship of You. Seeing You clearly means I see everything else clearly. Thank You, my Father. Amen.

A desire to worship

FOR READING & MEDITATION – PSALM 29:1–11

'worship the LORD in the splendour of his holiness.' (v2)

People have asked me the question: 'Do you find it possible to turn your heart in worship towards God when things go terribly wrong in your life?' My answer is this: 'I find it difficult, but not impossible.' It may seem that we are not as far along the road of discipleship as others, but if we are finding it easier to turn to God in worship when things in our lives are upside down than it was, say, ten years ago – then at least it shows we are making progress. It is something that comes more readily with practice.

When my wife died, I found it exceedingly difficult to put together words that would constitute any kind of worshipful prayer as I knelt before the Almighty. Yet I found that though words seemed to freeze on my lips, my heart still wanted to worship Him. When I sensed that, I knew that I had gone deeper with God than I realised. The pain of bereavement had a numbing effect on me (that in itself was not a negative thing), but within my soul I recognised a desire to worship.

FURTHER STUDY

Psa. 109:1–31; 136:1–26

1. What were some of the psalmist's difficult experiences?

2. What was his response and conviction?

The whole matter comes back to what I was saying earlier concerning the character of God. If we have doubts about His character, then we will not want to worship Him. We are made in such a way that we cannot give ourselves to anyone we doubt. Thus if we say to ourselves in the midst of disorder and disaster, 'God is not good in letting this happen to me', then worship will be almost impossible. Rather, let's turn to God and say, 'Lord, I don't understand why this is happening to me, but I know that You are good and that in all things You work for the good of those who love You (Rom. 8:28). I will drop my anchor in that great fact.'

Father, how I long to reach the place where, no matter what happens to me, my heart responds in praise and adoration of You. Help me, dear Father. In Jesus' name. Amen.

A good and forgiving God

FOR READING & MEDITATION – HEBREWS 10:19–31

'let us draw near to God with a sincere heart in full assurance of faith' (v22)

Today we try to understand the concept that lies behind the word 'worship'. The essential meaning of the word, both in the Old and New Testaments, is that of reverential service. Our present-day English word has evolved from the Anglo-Saxon *weorthscipe*, which means to give worth to something. Worship, as preachers and Bible teachers are quick to highlight, means worth-ship – to give worth to something or someone.

This thought, of course, is reflected everywhere in the Scriptures, such as the opening of the Lord's Prayer. We see it clearly in the passage before us today. True worship of God happens when a person draws near to God with 'a sincere heart in full assurance of faith', believing, indeed knowing, that He is there, and that He is a good and forgiving God, and ascribing to Him the honour and worth that is due to His name.

Archbishop William Temple, the Anglican theologian, wrote some words concerning worship, which I consider to be among the most beautiful I have ever read: 'Worship is the submission of all our nature to God. It is the quickening of conscience by His holiness, the nourishment of mind with His truth, the purifying of imagination by His beauty, the opening of the heart to love, the surrender of will to His purpose – and all this is gathered up in adoration to the most selfless emotion of which our nature is capable, and therefore the chief remedy for that self-centredness, which is the original sin and the source of all actual sin.'

Let's always remember that in worshipping God we are not demeaned but developed. We were made for worship. In glorifying God we complete ourselves.

FURTHER STUDY

Psa. 73:1–28; 145:1–21

1. What did the psalmist say was good for him?

2. What reasons did the psalmist give for worshipping God?

Dear Father, help me draw near to You now 'with a sincere heart in full assurance of faith'. Help me to submit all of my nature to You when I worship. In Jesus' name. Amen.

Tuning our instruments

FOR READING & MEDITATION – PSALM 50:1–23

*'If I were hungry I would not tell you, for the world is mine,
and all that is in it.' (v12)*

I wonder, have you ever been troubled by the kind of thoughts that occurred to me during the early days of my Christian experience concerning this matter of the worship of God? My question was why God put so many texts and references in the Bible that command us to worship Him. It seemed to me that many of these commands bordered on vanity and self-centredness. We all struggle with people who clamour for our attention or commendation, and a picture of a God who needed constant ego strokes threatened to impress itself on my mind. It happened most when I read the Psalms. 'Praise me, worship me' – it seemed that God was saying it everywhere.

When I read C.S. Lewis' *Reflections on the Psalms* I experienced a 'eureka' moment. The light of my understanding came on. He said: 'The miserable idea that God should in any sense need, or crave for, our worship like a vain woman wanting compliments, or a vain author presenting his new books to people who had never met or heard of him, is implicitly answered by the words: "If I be hungry I will not tell *thee*" (Psa. 50:12). Even if such an absurd Deity could be conceived, He would hardly come to *us*, the lowest of rational creatures, to gratify His appetite. I don't want my dog to bark approval of my books.'

Lewis said that in commanding us to worship Him, God is demonstrating far more interest in us than in Himself. Our worship of Him completes and perfects us. In eternity we will experience full joy, because we shall be able to worship Him fully. Meanwhile, we are tuning our instruments.

FURTHER STUDY

1 Chron. 16:8–36;
Rev. 4:8–11;
5:11–13

1. What is the anthem of heaven?

2. Why not echo the anthem yourself today.

Mighty God, I want to worship You in truth and for all that You are. Help me give You my worship not because I am completed by it, but because You are so worthy of it. I worship You, Father, with all my heart. Amen.

Worship (really) is central

FOR READING & MEDITATION – PSALM 132:1–18

'Let us go to his dwelling-place; let us worship at his footstool' (v7)

We spend one more day meditating on the suggestion that if we are to pursue God and go deeper with Him, then it's important we learn to understand both the importance and meaning of worship. Dr Dick Averby, an Old Testament scholar and professor, suggests that the antidote to every human problem is worship. I am sure he is thinking of personality problems, not physical problems, and allowing for this caveat, I would agree with him. Dr Larry Crabb, of New Way Ministries based in Colorado, USA, says something similar: 'Worship means, in the middle of life as it is experienced, that you find some way to be caught up in God's character and purpose so that His will becomes central.'

FURTHER STUDY

1 Cor. 1:1–17;
Acts 3:11–16;
14:11–15

1. What was a problem in the Early Church?

2. How did Peter and John deal with this problem?

Mature Christians, who know what it means to have a deep and ongoing relationship with God, are people who think of themselves first and foremost as worshippers. They will see their other roles in life – as fathers, mothers, factory workers, business people, farmers, doctors, mechanics, teachers, and so on – as secondary.

Some worship the servants of God more than they worship God Himself. A story is told of an occasion when Christmas Evans, the great Welsh preacher of a past century, was due to preach at a certain church. Prior to the service, the church was packed with people eager to hear him. As the service was about to begin, it was announced that Christmas Evans was unable to keep the engagement and a lesser-known preacher would take his place. People began to show signs of leaving until the moderator said: 'All those who have come to worship Christmas Evans may leave. All those who have come to worship God may stay.' No one left.

My Father and my God, may this emphasis on worship remain undiminished as I turn to other things. I see it is so central. Help me not only to remember it but to apply it. In Jesus' name. Amen.

Spiritual passion

FOR READING & MEDITATION – PSALM 63:1–11

*'O God, you are my God, earnestly I seek you; my soul thirsts for you,
my body longs for you' (v1)*

A further issue we must face if we are to go deeper with God is the need to understand the importance of pursuing Him with passion. Here I am talking about something much greater than spending time with Him, but allowing the deep thirsts and longings for God that He has built into our souls to find their freest and fullest expression.

One of the saddest things to come across in the Christian Church is the attitude that says: 'I have found God so there is no longer any need to pursue Him.' To have found God and yet be filled with an immense desire to pursue Him is one of the great paradoxes of the Christian life. Such an idea is disparaged by the easily satisfied religionist, who seeks for nothing more than a guarantee of heaven. The paradox of which I am now talking is expressed most powerfully by St Bernard of Clairvaux:

> *We taste Thee, O Thou living Bread,*
> *And long to feast upon Thee still;*
> *We drink of Thee, the Fountainhead,*
> *And thirst our souls from Thee to fill.*

FURTHER STUDY

Isa. 55:1–9;
Psa. 42:1–2;
38:9; 73:25

1. How did Isaiah express his longing for the Lord?

2. What conclusion did the psalmist come to?

One of the pitfalls of contemporary Christianity is that so many of Christ's followers are too easily satisfied. They drink from the Fountainhead, and seem to be so satisfied with what they have received that they have no desire to drink more. They do not understand the paradox that to drink the water that Jesus provides is to be satisfied, but satisfied with an unsatisfied satisfaction.

**Father, can it be that in spiritual things I am too easily satisfied?
That I am content with what I have and do not seek for more?
Help me search my heart as I ponder this issue day by day.
In Jesus' name I pray. Amen.**

The soul's paradox

FOR READING & MEDITATION – MATTHEW 6:25–34

'But seek first his kingdom and his righteousness' (v33)

We move very carefully now, as I am dealing with issues that can easily be misunderstood. They are so crucial, however, that the failure to understand them can hinder us in our quest to pursue and go deeper with God. Yesterday we ended with the paradoxical thought that when we come to Jesus, we are satisfied with an unsatisfied satisfaction. Jesus most certainly quenches our soul's great thirst, but in quenching it He arouses within us the thirst for more. Many in today's Church do not understand this paradox, and as a consequence are spiritually poor. 'To have found God and still to pursue Him,' said St Bernard of Clairvaux (whose poetic lines we referred to yesterday), 'is the soul's paradox of love.'

FURTHER STUDY

Luke 6:17–21;
Psa. 143:6;
84:1–2

1. What is promised to those who hunger?

2. How did the psalmist describe his thirst?

When considering this, I checked my dictionary to remind myself of the meaning of the word 'paradox'. The word means a seemingly absurd though perhaps actually well-founded statement. To say that God satisfies but leaves us thirsting for more seems absurd, but I suggest it is nevertheless 'a well-founded statement'. Although it seems contradictory, the more one ponders it, the more one comes to see it is true.

Some people don't like to struggle with paradoxes; they prefer what they describe as 'simple logic'. When I was in Malaysia once, a man said to me: 'I am grateful I've found Christ, but it seems logical now to pursue my career with all the energy I possess and leave the knowledge of God until I get to heaven.' I felt deeply saddened in my spirit as I heard this. It is not wrong to pursue one's career or other interests, but as the verse before us today makes clear – not at the expense of pursuing God.

Gracious and loving heavenly Father, I have tasted deeply of You but yet my soul longs for more. Lead me on my Father. I ask for more and more and more. Amen.

How wonderful...

FOR READING & MEDITATION – EXODUS 33:12–23

'Then Moses said, "Now show me your glory."' (v18)

The kind of reasoning we have been exploring over the past couple of days that says, 'Now I have found God there is no reason to seek Him further' is not found anywhere in the Scriptures. Both Old and New Testaments are replete with instances of those who, having come to know God, longed to know Him better. The passage before us today provides us with one such example.

Moses is not content with having come to know God well; he uses the fact that he has entered into a relationship with God as an argument for knowing Him more deeply. Listen to how the Living Bible puts it: 'You say you are my friend, and that I have found favour before you; please, if this is really so, guide me clearly along the way you want me to travel so that I will understand you and walk acceptably before you' (v12). That is the kind of bold and powerful praying that someone who longs after God with great passion will undertake. Later, he makes the audacious request that forms the words of our text for today, and this issue's key verse: 'Now show me your glory.' Do you not sense in those words the heart and passion of a man with an intense desire to know God better? Clearly God was contented with Moses' request, for He invites him to come up the Mount the very next day, where He reveals His glory to him.

How amazing it would be today if we were gripped by such an overwhelming desire to know God better, to taste more of Him, to feel Him at work more powerfully in our souls, to see Him as Moses did with our inner eyes, that we turn from this moment and find some quiet spot where we too will pray: 'Lord God, show me Your glory.'

FURTHER STUDY

Phil. 3:1–11;
Hosea 6:3;
Col. 1:10

1. What was Paul's great desire?

2. What lengths was he prepared to go to?

Father, show me Your glory, and begin in me this day a deeper work of love than ever before. In Christ's name. Amen.

Only an appetiser

FOR READING & MEDITATION – PSALM 27:1–14

'My heart says of you, "Seek his face!" Your face, LORD, I will seek.'
(v8)

Yesterday we looked at God's servant, Moses, whose pursuit to know God more closely led him to pray the most audacious of prayers: 'Now show me your glory.' One of the things that characterises the godly men and women in Scripture is the passion of their pursuit of God. King David is another example. Though he was guilty of two devastating sins – murder and adultery – it is clear that he yearned after God, and longed for Him with intense spiritual passion. His psalms ring with the cry of the seeker and the glad shout of the finder. But even when he finds Him, his heart is eager to know more.

FURTHER STUDY

John 6:25–58;
Isa. 55:2;
1 Cor. 10:3–4

1. What did Jesus declare?

2. Why did the Jews stumble over it?

The same longing can be seen in the life of the apostle Paul – one of the most outstanding Christians in history. Has anyone known God more intimately than he did? Yet this is his plea in the letter he wrote to the Philippians: 'That I may know him, and the power of his resurrection' (Phil. 3:10, AV). He did know Him, but his plea is that he might know Him more.

'Today we have most of our seeking done for us by devotional writers,' said a critic of daily devotional aids in a recent magazine article. 'They set out what we should think about in our quiet times.' In part, I feel he is right. I tell you, if you are satisfied with this devotional and do not go beyond it to seek God for yourself, then you are spiritually too easily satisfied. *Every Day with Jesus* is meant to be a spiritual primer, not a satisfier; an appetiser, not the feast. The longings God has put within your soul for Him can be met only by Him. If these writings help you draw closer to Him, that's wonderful. But if they don't, do find a way.

Lord God, human words can inspire but only Your words can feed me. May I continually seek You. Amen.

CWR

Pursuing God
...through courses, events and seminars

'The course expanded my knowledge, which I've found makes Bible reading even more exciting and enlivening!'
– The Life and Times of Jesus course delegate

Understanding who we are in God transforms how we live out our lives. This is why the Bible is at the heart of all our teaching. CWR's courses cover many different areas of life, faith and ministry – from insight into issues such as bereavement or anxiety, to women's ministry and team leadership. We can also bring seminars to your church or group. Visit the website to discover more.

www.cwr.org.uk/courses

There's more!

FOR READING & MEDITATION – PSALM 143:1–12

'my soul thirsts for you like a parched land.' (v6)

We continue reflecting on the fact that those who know God intimately pursue Him with passion. A noticeable flaw in contemporary discipleship is the absence of passion.

A.W. Tozer suggested that one 'thermometer' for measuring the health of the Church of his day was its current songs and literature. He went on to say that comparison of songs and writings with those of, say, even 50 years previously revealed a marked difference in the mood of the Church. In times past people's thoughts were preoccupied with knowing God more deeply. Today (and I emphasise this is only a generalisation) the focus is on what we have already found in God. I cast my mind back and think of the songs I sang as a youth, which had lines like these: 'His track I see and I'll pursue', or 'My soul follows on hard after Thee.' Are these same sentiments to be found in contemporary songs? Not to the same degree, it seems. Of course, we rejoice in what we have found in God, but let's not lose sight of the fact that there's more.

FURTHER STUDY

Eph. 3:14–21;
1 Chron. 28:9;
Psa. 100:3

1. What does Paul pray the Ephesians will come to know more?

2. What was David's admonition to Solomon?

It is the same with contemporary Christian literature. Again, this is only a generalisation, but so much of today's writing is experience-oriented, and can lead to us seeking God not for who He is, but for what we can get out of Him. To know God and not to thirst to know Him more is rarely, as some might see it, a sign of spiritual satisfaction. Never be ashamed of your lack of satisfaction. To know God, to *really* know Him, is to be made more thirsty still. To quote Tozer again: 'Paul was a seeker and a finder, and a seeker still.'

Father, help me grasp this paradox that the more I am satisfied the more my soul yearns for greater things. Take me deeper into You, dear Father. Amen.

A deep thirst

FOR READING & MEDITATION – PSALM 42:1–11

*'As the deer pants for streams of water, so my soul pants for you,
O God.' (v1)*

It is time now to ask ourselves: Do we want more of God? Do we 'pant' after Him? The psalmist paints a vivid picture in the passage before us today of a deer panting for streams of water. Perhaps he had just seen such an animal being chased by a predator and, having escaped, desperately looking for water to quench its thirst. The Hebrew word for 'pant' literally means a desire so intense that it becomes audible. In presenting us with this picture the psalmist is, I think, intending to convey the impression that his longing after God was not some passing interest, but his chief objective. Nothing mattered more to him than the pursuit of God.

Panting presupposes a thirst. Are we thirsty for God to such a degree that we long after Him in the same way that a thirsty deer pants for water? The thirst for God is there in all of us, but the problem is that we do not sense that thirst. Prior to faith we either denied or suppressed it, or attempted to satisfy it in ways apart from God. In following Jesus we give up (to some degree at least) such things as denial, suppression and attempting to satisfy the ache in our soul through ways other than God, and we find ourselves getting more and more in touch with the desire for God that He has placed within us. This becomes evident when we realise that we want to read His Word and talk to Him in prayer. And sometimes the desire to do these things becomes stronger than almost anything we have ever experienced before.

Those who go deeper with God are those who know how to get in touch with the thirst that God has placed in the soul and allow it its full expression.

FURTHER STUDY

Psa. 63:1–11;
105:4;
119:20,131

1. How did David seek God?

2. How does the psalmist describe his inner passion?

Lord, if You have placed such a deep thirst in my soul, why do I not feel more thirsty for You? Take me through this issue to greater clarity and understanding. In Jesus' name. Amen.

Renouncing dependence

FOR READING & MEDITATION – JEREMIAH 2:1–14

*'My people... have forsaken me, the spring of living water,
and have dug their own cisterns' (v13)*

If God has placed within us a heart that 'pants' after Him, why do we not feel more thirsty than we do? What can we do to get in touch with the deep longing for God, which our creator has put at the very centre of our beings?

The major reason is the stubborn commitment to independence which, because of the Fall of mankind, characterises every one of us. We like to feel we are in control of the way our soul's thirst can be satisfied. In today's reading, we see Israel being charged with two evils – forsaking the spring of living water and digging their own cisterns for holding water. Why would they do such a thing – turning away from a fresh spring and digging cisterns, broken cisterns that could not hold water? Because they liked the feeling they got from seeking independently to find water for their souls.

FURTHER STUDY

Psa. 36:1–9;
46:4;
John 4:10;
7:37–38

1. Where can we drink from?

2. Where can we find its source?

The opposite of independence is dependence. And that is the main prerequisite if we are to utilise the great thirst that God has put within us. But giving up our independence and trusting God to come through for us is not easy. None of us likes giving up control. We all like being in the driving seat or say, as the poet W.E. Henley put it, 'I am the master of my fate. The captain of my soul', and to admit to helplessness, vulnerability, dependence, and having to place our trust in another are things that rankle within our proud personalities. It is our commitment to independence that prevents us from feeling what God has put deep within us. When we can learn to give up our independence and enter a life of trust, then our passion for God will not just be experienced in our soul, but explode in it.

Father, release me from my commitment to independence, and make me a more God-dependent person. In Jesus' name I pray. Amen.

God in His own community

FOR READING & MEDITATION – GENESIS 1:20–31

'Then God said, "Let us make man in our image, in our likeness"'
(v26)

I have come to the conclusion that in our pursuit of God one of the most important issues is relationships. Although at first it may not be obvious, as we explore the issue of relationships together over the next few days, I hope you too will begin to see why this is absolutely key. This was brought home to me while reading a book entitled *The Everlasting God*, written by the Anglican theologian, D. Broughton Knox.

In a chapter describing the Trinity, he clarifies that, fundamentally, God is a relational being. This is the truth being hinted at in our text for today, where we see that there is more than one divine person in the Godhead. God is a community – a community of three persons who relate to one another in perfect harmony. No quarrels, no arguments, no tensions. The Father loves the Son and gives Him everything (John 3:35). The Son always does that which pleases the Father (John 8:29). The Spirit takes the things of the Son and shows them to us (John 16:15).

FURTHER STUDY

John 5:16–23; 14:7–14

1. Why did the Jews try to kill Jesus?

2. How can we know the Father?

Broughton Knox made this statement in his book which, when I read it, brought about one of the greatest changes in my thinking I have ever experienced: 'We learn from the Trinity that relationship is the essence of reality… and therefore the essence of our existence.' Up until that moment I had always believed that the ultimate reality was truth. But I came to see that important though truth is, it is not the ultimate reality. Truth is propositional; relationship is personal. When you touch the heart of the universe you touch not simply an idea, a law or even a thought. You touch a God who relates. There is warmth, not just wonder, at the heart of the Trinity – the warmth of interpersonal relationships.

God my Father, help me to realise the truth that You are a relational God. I long to pursue a relationship with every part of who You are. In Jesus' name. Amen.

Nothing more important

FOR READING & MEDITATION – HEBREWS 8:1–13

'I will be their God, and they will be my people.' (v10)

Today we continue thinking about the Trinity and relationships. In some religions God is presented as a solitary figure – a God who needs nobody, feels nothing, but just sits and thinks. In others there is a vast hierarchy of independent gods either fighting one another or doing their own thing. The biblical view of the Trinity cuts right across these false ideas. It presents the truth of one God in three persons – Father, Son and Holy Spirit – who exist in mutual love and understanding.

FURTHER STUDY

Matt. 28:18–19;
2 Cor. 13:11–14;
1 Pet. 1:2

1. How did Jesus and Peter show their awareness of the Trinity?

2. What does Paul's blessing reveal about the Trinity?

'If we believe that God exists eternally in three persons,' says one author, 'who are distinct enough to relate to one another, then it becomes clear that somehow final reality is wrapped up in the idea of relationship.' God experienced love within Himself before the world was created. The doctrine of the Trinity establishes the fact that relationship is not simply the essence of God's being, but the foundation for everything. God's covenant with Israel, as we see from today's reading, provided for an agreement and a harmonious relationship. And the Son of God was sent to restore humanity to a harmonious relationship (John 3:16).

This relational quality that we see in the Trinity – and this is my main point – is expected also of the people God has created. When Jesus was asked to identify the greatest commandment, He selected these two: 'Love the Lord your God with all your heart and with all your soul and with all your mind' and 'Love your neighbour as yourself' (Matt. 22:36–39). In other words, loving relationships – love of God and love of others – is what life is all about. Nothing is more important.

Father, forgive us, Your Church, for putting our programmes, our schedules, even the size of our congregations, before the quality of our relationships. Help us see that our greatest calling is to be people who love. In Jesus' name. Amen.

Other-centredness

FOR READING & MEDITATION – JOHN 13:18–38

'Love one another. As I have loved you, so you must love one another.'
(v34)

It is clear that God places a high value on relationships. As the Welsh preacher Dr Cynddylan Jones said: 'The best way in which we, the people of God, can reflect the nature of God here on earth is in the way we relate.' But what does it mean to relate well? How do we define a good relationship?

A good relationship exists when we are using our resources for the wellbeing of others. Listen to Broughton Knox again as he expands his ideas concerning the Trinity: 'We learn from the Trinity that the way relationship should be expressed is by concern for others. Within the Trinity itself there is a concern by each member for the others.'

Clearly, then, the energy and strength that pulses in the heart of the Trinity is other-centred. By that I mean it is turned outwards, not inwards. This is why self-centredness is such a damaging attitude; it breaks the very order of the universe. God created (and then recreated) us to relate well to Him and relate well to others. He meant us first to enjoy Him, and then to reflect His character by giving ourselves unselfishly to one another.

However, something has gone wrong. Most of us have to admit that we are far more concerned about ourselves than we are about others. There are times, of course, when that is not so – when we reach out to others and think more of them and their interests than we do of ourselves and our own agenda. But how many of us can claim that we are consistently other-centred? I know I can't. How about you? I think that as I have grown older my self-centredness has diminished, but there is still too much for a child of God.

FURTHER STUDY

Rom. 14:15;
15:1–7;
Phil. 2:1–8

1. In what practical ways can we show love to each other?

2. How did Christ model other-centredness?

Gracious and loving God, You who relate in glorious other-centredness, help me to do the same. May self-centredness be rooted out of me. In Jesus' name I pray. Amen.

Partner with us

as we pursue God together

Throughout this issue, we have highlighted the main areas of CWR's work and ministry. We hope that you will continue to be blessed and encouraged by *Every Day with Jesus*. And you can pass that blessing on by getting involved! With the prayers and financial help of CWR's Partners, we can reach more people with life-changing teaching, training, books and resources.

As a Partner, you will enable...

...the development of Bible reading notes for future generations

'*Every Day with Jesus* has definitely played a huge part in my Christian growth. I look forward to every issue, mark them, keep them and encourage my friends to read them.'

...more than 60,000 resources being sent into prisons in the UK and Australia every year
'Daily readings are an important part of my faith here and I only wish I had read more in the past. God is truly blessing me with freedom, despite being behind bars.'

...people to receive invaluable teaching by subsidising the costs of our courses
'After attending an Inspiring Women weekend course, I feel more of God's love, and know that I have crossed a line from the past and am now looking to the future.'

...the creation of Bible-based resources for children
'*Topz* shows me how God and Jesus are so important to us all. Now I really enjoy being a Christian. I hope everybody loves *Topz* the way I do!'

Join in and help others pursue God through all areas of our ministry. Get in touch to find out more.
Email **partners@cwr.org.uk** or call **01252 784709** or visit the website today.

www.cwr.org.uk/partners

'Another gospel'

FOR READING & MEDITATION – 1 JOHN 4:13–21

'We love because he first loved us.' (v19)

God has a very simple pattern for our relationships. First we relate to Him, then to others, and we ourselves come last. But I fear that 'another gospel' is gaining acceptance in the Christian community that changes that order around. Attention is focused on loving ourselves so that then, it is said, we are better able to love God and love others. One Christian author wrote: 'Until you learn to love yourself you can't love others and you can't love God. So concentrate on enjoying your value as a person, and the more you come to appreciate this the more you will be able to reach out to God and to others.'

FURTHER STUDY

Rom. 5:1–8;
1 Pet. 1:8–9,
18–23

1. Where does love originate?

2. What should we do with the love we have received?

Some of you may be wondering what bothers me about this. Let me try to explain: it is the complete opposite of the biblical pattern. The biblical model is that first we relate to God by asking Him to forgive our sins. The moment He does this, He pours in His love which, in turn, as our text for today tells us, creates within us a love for Him. Now notice this: it is His love for us that causes our hearts to respond in love to Him. Our love for Him is thus the response to His love for us. It is not something manufactured or concocted; His *agape* produces *agape* in us. Having been filled with God's love, we are then to give ourselves to others with an energy that longs to see the same confidence we have in God grow and develop in them.

Lastly, remember that we rejoice in who we are, and enjoy our identity as children of the King. Our value as men and women comes from the truth that God lives in us and loves in us, and that we have something useful to give to others. Freely we have received, freely we give.

Father, forgive me when I reverse the divine order for relationships by putting myself ahead of others – and perhaps even You. Impress the proper order into my spirit: You first, others second, myself last. In Jesus' name. Amen.

The best X-ray

FOR READING & MEDITATION – COLOSSIANS 3:1–17

'*clothe yourselves with compassion, kindness, humility,
gentleness and patience.*' (v12)

The conviction that the matter of relationships is a key issue in the universe has deepened within me over the years. All biblical history is a record of God calling individuals and communities of people to a relationship with Him, because that is the supreme purpose of life. As we saw earlier, the Shorter Westminster Catechism states: 'The chief end of man[kind] is to glorify God and to enjoy him for ever' (a statement based on 1 Cor. 10:31 and Psa. 73:25–26). We are designed to worship and relate, and when our relationships are loving and other-centred, we reflect the design of the Trinity in the highest and most glorious way possible.

FURTHER STUDY

Gal. 5:13–26;
1 John 3:11–20

1. How does our attitude to others reveal our hearts?

2. How can we know that God's love is in us?

The Bible is a manual intended to help us discover the true purpose of life and to grow in it. Have you ever wondered why there are so many accounts of relationships in the Bible? It is crammed with stories of people relating well or not relating well. The content of the Bible is not only propositional, it is also relational.

Now let me go a stage further and say something that might surprise you. Almost every problem we have in life (if it is not biological) will stem from a difficulty in relationships – our relationship with God, with others or with ourselves. Our relationships probably give the best X-ray of the condition of our soul, for our true dedication to God will show itself in the way we relate to Him, to others and to ourselves. Remember, we are not mechanical beings – we are personal, made in God's image. That means there is always something going on between us and others. And, if we are truly His, what goes on should reflect His attitude towards us.

Father, if it is true that my relationships give the best X-ray of my soul then help me examine myself in Your presence. Help me to answer the question: Do I reach out to others in the same way that You reach out to me? Amen.

Love never fails

FOR READING & MEDITATION – MATTHEW 10:1–16

'Freely you have received, freely give.' (v8)

I am persuaded that, in every situation, to act with love makes the best sense. It is, as someone has described it, the only realism. To act with anything other than love is to inject into every relationship a disruptive tendency, which will sooner or later create chaos. It is my belief that, inherently, everything is made to work in love's way, and in no other way. If we try to make life work in any way other than in love then, though it may seem to work, in reality it is working to its own ruin.

This is not to say that the people to whom we show love will respond to that love. Love will not necessarily bring about what it longs to achieve. When Paul said 'Love never fails' (1 Cor. 13:8) he did not mean that love will always succeed in gaining its object. In that respect it can fail. He meant that even though you may not succeed in a situation when acting upon love, nevertheless you have not failed, for you yourself are better for acting in that way.

FURTHER STUDY

Phil. 1:1–11;
2 Thess. 1:1–3

1. What did Paul pray for?

2. Why did Paul thank God?

In today's passage we see Jesus telling His disciples to offer peace to a house. If the people of the house received it, well and good. If they did not receive it then the disciples were exhorted to let the peace return to them. They themselves were more peaceful for having given the peace – so in either case they win. It is the same also with us. If we give love and people receive it, then good. If they don't take it, it is still good. Heads we win, tails we also win. The loving person always wins, for he or she becomes more loving in giving out love, even if the other person doesn't accept it. 'Love never fails.' It never fails to enrich the giver, for the more love he or she gives, the more love they can receive, to give again.

Father, I accept that to love is always the right thing to do. Since I am willing to love, please empower me so that my love will grow stronger and stronger. In Jesus' name I ask this. Amen.

Unlove cannot succeed

FOR READING & MEDITATION – 1 CORINTHIANS 16:5–18

'Do everything in love.' (v14)

The thought with which we ended yesterday was that love cannot fail. It is true also to say that the unloving act cannot succeed. If we appear to succeed in accomplishing things by an unloving attitude the success is not real, since the unloving attitude or deed – like a loving attitude or deed – registers itself within us. Our whole being is demeaned by unloving behaviour. If love never fails, then unlove never succeeds. It cannot by its very nature. This is why we must bestow love, for we are made by the very qualities we exhibit.

But is this a practicable way to live? Won't people take advantage of us? Our calling as Christians is to do what is right and leave the consequences to God. Only as Jesus is allowed to live in us will we find it possible to love. For it is His love working through us that produces the victory.

A professor of psychiatry recalled how one day he asked his students to write down the initials of the people they most disliked. After a minute, some had as many as 20 sets of initials, while others could think of only one person's initials. He made this interesting comment: 'The people with the longest lists were among the most unpopular on the campus.' When I read that I was reminded of Benjamin Franklin's famous words, 'To be loved you have to be lovable.'

May I suggest, then, that you make this a life goal: 'Love shall always be my method of living while I am here on this earth.' And what about when you get to heaven? You need not concern yourself about that for, as one person has commented, 'Love is the climate of heaven.' There, love is practised to perfection.

FURTHER STUDY

John 13:34–35;
Rom. 13:8–10;
Eph. 4:31–5:2

1. Why does love fulfil the law?

2. How should we imitate Christ?

Father, I see that the closer I get to Jesus, the better I will love. Help me to do everything through love, for love, and by love. And may I be more concerned about giving love than receiving it. In Jesus' name. Amen.

The art of loving

FOR READING & MEDITATION – ROMANS 13:1–10

'Let no debt remain outstanding, except the continuing debt to love one another' (v8)

Relationships are more easily talked about than entered into. As a young Christian, I regarded other people as the cause of many of my problems. But then I realised that relationships do not so much cause problems as reveal problems. The problems in my relationships were caused not so much by the way others treated me, but by the way I reacted to them. The major problem was not other people, but me. One of the greatest challenges of my life has been to consider others more important than me. Nowhere do I have a greater opportunity to demonstrate other-centredness than in my relationships – in moving in love to those I might even dislike.

FURTHER STUDY

Eph. 4:11–16; Col. 3:12–17

1. What contributes to our unity and to our maturity?

2. Describe the lifestyle of God's chosen people.

Dr E. Stanley Jones defined Christianity as 'the science of relating well to others in the spirit of Jesus Christ'. He also said 'we are as mature as our relationships'. Unless we learn to relate to others in the way that the Trinity relates to each other – in other-centredness – we may well find our union with God somewhat blocked.

C.S. Lewis said the Church is a laboratory in which we have the opportunity to fine-tune our relationships. There we learn to love as we have been loved. As we come in contact with people we have an opportunity to practise the art of loving which, as we saw earlier, is of the essence of reality. We are to relate to people, not on the basis of how they relate to us, but on how Christ relates to us. 'Love one another. As I have loved you, so you must love one another,' Jesus instructed (John 13:34). This is another vital element of our spiritual journey. We are to love others as we love ourselves. And, as we do so, we will find we are moving closer to God.

Gracious Lord, if it is true that I am as mature as my relationships, help me to make my relationship with You the strongest relationship in my life. For then I know that everything good will follow. Amen.

Next Issue

MAR/APR 2018

A Higher Love

Underpinning the universe is a passionate purpose. God is inviting us into an intimate relationship with Him. In this issue, Selwyn unpacks a theme that is brought out in Scripture over and over again – the passionate yet tender love that lies at the heart of the Trinity.

This Easter time, explore how the cross is our anchor, and how we have been created in such a way that only God can truly satisfy, comfort and guide us – no matter what we face in life.

Every Day
with Jesus
MAR/APR 2018

A Higher Love

'Many waters cannot
quench love; rivers cannot
wash it away.'
Song of Songs 8:7

Living life with Jesus. Every day   **CWR**

**Also available as eBook/
eSubscription**

**Obtain your copy from CWR,
a Christian bookshop or your
National Distributor.**
If you would like to take out a
subscription, see the order form
at the back of these notes.

Last, but not least

FOR READING & MEDITATION – 1 SAMUEL 15:10–23

'To obey is better than sacrifice, and to heed is better than the fat of rams.' (v22)

We come now to the last matter we must make a priority if we are to pursue God. I am sure it goes without saying that the priorities we have discussed are not the only matters we should consider if we want to develop a closer relationship with God. They are, however, in my opinion, some of the foremost. The final issue I want to look at is this – the necessity of obedience. The moment we stop obeying God is the moment we stop moving on with Him. We move along the road to a deeper experience of God in relation (as we have seen) to many things, and obedience, though listed last, is certainly not the least in importance. It stands shoulder to shoulder with the other priorities and is equal in significance to every one of them.

FURTHER STUDY

Josh. 1:1–8; 11:15; 24:31

1. What did God promise to Joshua as a result of obedience?

2. What epitaph is recorded of Joshua?

In the passage before us today we see Samuel going to the very heart of the issue with which King Saul struggled – the desire to go his own way instead of being willing to take God's way. Saul's great sin was that he did not take God seriously. He disobeyed the divine command to destroy all the Amalekites and saved Agag, their king, from the sword. He probably said to himself: 'As long as I obey most of God's commands then He will overlook the one I don't obey.' When we start such a process of rationalisation we do not know where it will end. For Saul, it ended in destruction. No matter how many sacrifices he offered, they could never make up for his deliberate disobedience. When God asks us to obey, we follow His instructions – for no amount of attendance at church services, prayer meetings, or Bible reading can compensate for the sin of deliberate, continued disobedience.

Lord God, reveal to me any areas of my life where I have been continually disobedient. Help me to be true to You. In Jesus' name. Amen.

Futile striving

FOR READING & MEDITATION – JUDGES 16:1–22

'But he did not know that the LORD had left him.' (v20)

Which of us has not struggled to obey something that God has asked us to do? Perhaps you couldn't see the reason for it, or it didn't seem to make sense. Yet as you thought about the matter, you decided to obey anyway, simply because God asked it of you. There is, however, a big difference between the struggles that are fairly soon overcome and continued disobedience. Christians who continue to wilfully and deliberately ignore the clear instructions and guidelines outlined in Scripture will never, no matter how much they throw themselves into Christian activity, experience the fullness of fellowship with God.

FURTHER STUDY

Deut. 5:1–29;
1 Kings 3:14;
1 Sam. 12:15;
James 1:25;
Eph. 5:6

1. What was God's desire for His people?

2. What is the result of disobedience?

Over the years I have known a few Christian leaders who became involved in extramarital affairs and have claimed: 'God doesn't seem to mind as much about this as His people might if they knew, as He appears to bless my preaching more than ever.' This was a rationalisation. They were like Samson who, as we see from today's passage, thought to himself: 'Everything is fine. I'll go out and shake myself.' But he did not know, the Scripture tells us, 'that the LORD had left him'. The reason why such people appear to be blessed could be because unconsciously they put more of themselves into their messages in an effort to compensate for the feelings of guilt deep inside them. However, the consequences of their actions always catch up.

Sadly, we lack the same sensitivity to the Spirit that was present in the Early Church, when such things would have been quickly spotted and exposed. Preachers can shake, shout, shriek, and perspire as they preach, but it is all meaningless if there is no obedience.

Father, save me from focusing on the disobedience of others and overlooking the faults of my own heart. Help me understand what Saul seemed to misunderstand – that without obedience there is no meaning. In Christ's name I pray. Amen.

'The Way' – unqualified

FOR READING & MEDITATION – ACTS 9:1–19

*'if he found any there who belonged to the Way,
whether men or women' (v2)*

In my pursuit of God, I've discovered that God's way is the only way that works. Jesus talked about two ways: the way that leads to destruction, and the way that leads to life (Matt. 7:13–14). When we accept God's gift of salvation, made possible by Jesus' death on the cross, then we find ourselves on the way leading to life.

In the text for today we read of those who belonged to 'the Way' – way with a capital 'W'. Just three or four years after the crucifixion – and before they were called 'Christians' – this is how believers were being described. So why were

FURTHER STUDY

Isa. 35:3–10;
Acts 18:24–28

1. Who could walk Isaiah's way?

2. What did Apollos need?

Jesus' followers first called people of 'the Way'? The early Christians no doubt recalled Jesus' declaration found in John 14:6 – 'I am the way and the truth and the life. No-one comes to the Father except through me' – and were absolutely clear that the message they proclaimed made known the only way to God. But 'the Way' signifies more than the way of salvation. It encompasses the whole of life – moral and spiritual.

The first Christians were aware of this, and not only believed something new but behaved in a manner that was new. In *The Call to Conversion*, Jim Wallis writes: 'Their faith produced a discernible lifestyle, a way of life... Christian belief became identified with a certain kind of behaviour.'

'The Way' is the way unqualified. It is the way to do everything – to think, to feel, to act, to conduct oneself in every possible circumstance. It is the way written into everything – the only way that works. All alternatives to the Way turn out to be ways to ruin. There are many wrong ways, but only one right way. Life, to me, is one long corroboration of that fact.

Father, to live Your way is life – and life abundant. To live in some other way is to experience death and disappointment. I am so grateful I have discovered this. Thank You, my Father. Amen.

The nature of reality

SUN
25 FEB

FOR READING & MEDITATION – JOHN 1:1–18

'Through him all things were made; without him nothing was made'
(v3)

We continue focusing on the fact that God's way is 'the Way', and all other ways are not the way. Is this arrogance? Some might think so, but actually it is the nature of reality. When God, in Christ, made all things, He made them to work in a certain way, and that way is Christ's way.

Today's text shows us that God created the world through Christ. Not only did He redeem the world through Christ, He created it through Him. In *The Message*, this verse reads: 'Everything was created through him; nothing – not one thing! – came into being without him.' This means, I believe, that all creation has the stamp of Jesus upon it. His will has been worked into its very structure. Creation was made by Him and for Him, Paul tells us in Colossians 1:16. By Him and for Him. The touch of Christ is on creation, and His purpose is moulded into creation. If it doesn't work for Him, then it works towards its own ruin.

God's way is not just written about in the Scriptures, it is written into the whole of the created universe. If 'the Way' was set forth only in the Scriptures, then a battle would be precipitated concerning the authority of the Scriptures – their authority and worth. The foundation of authority would be confined to the Bible; it would not be broadly based in the nature of reality. But 'the Way' is written into the nature of reality as well as into the Scriptures – thus 'the Way' is inescapable for everybody. 'The Way' is not a side issue or a matter for debate. It is the central issue of life. If you could split open creation you would find imprinted into it like a watermark, 'Made by Him and for Him.' Christ is the reality by whom all other reality is measured.

FURTHER STUDY

Psa. 19:1–6; John 14:1–7

1. What does creation declare?

2. Why are Christians often perceived as judgmental?

God, I am so thankful that I belong to 'the Way' – inherently. And 'the Way' belongs to me – inherently. Therefore we belong to each other – inherently. How glad I am that I entered into this inheritance when I entered into Christ. Amen.

The great design

FOR READING & MEDITATION – PROVERBS 14:1–18

*'The faithless will be fully repaid for their ways,
and the good man rewarded for his.' (v14)*

Can what we are talking about be really so – that all of life comes down to the fact that there is 'the Way' and not-the-way, and that we have a choice between 'the Way' and not-the-way? I am convinced it does. That choice confronts us in every thought, in every act, in every feeling, indeed, every time we do anything.

As an observer of human life in all its aspects, I am drawn inescapably to the conclusion that God's way is always the right way to do anything, and any other way is always the wrong way. When people live in a manner that goes against or resists the great design, they have to face the consequences; when they live in accordance with the great design, they gain its benefits. Sadly, there are no exceptions to this. As a counsellor, I have sat with people and seen them struggle while they tried to take not-the-way. Then I have rejoiced as they have come back and confessed that 'the Way' is the only way.

FURTHER STUDY

Prov. 2:6–22;
1 Tim. 6:6–10

1. What is the promise to those who follow the Lord?

2. Why may people become hurt in life?

Mice being used in a scientific experiment learn the way to the cheese by discovering that when they start going down a dead end, their noses get an electric shock. Something similar happens with human beings. They go down a route that looks as if it might take them to happiness, but then they get a shock that tells them this is not the right way. So they hunt around, looking for a shockless way. But there are no shockless ways. The shocks people receive don't always show up on their faces, but they certainly show up in the soul. 'The best teacher,' it has been said, 'is time.' Time inevitably renders a conclusion. It is sad when the conclusion is that a person is going down the wrong route.

Father, I see that life works in one way only – Your way. Help me take that way in everything. For Jesus' sake. Amen.

God's wise ways

'Each of you should look not only to your own interests,
but also to the interests of others.' (v4)

One thing that has fascinated me over the years is to see how people, by observation and experimentation, stumble on the truth that is written both in the Scriptures and the universe, namely that God's way is the right way and the only way. Let me give you some examples.

One expert on family relations says: 'You must give up yourself. You must serve others or you cannot get along with others.' Here is someone not of faith recognising that self-centredness is not-the-way – a spiritual issue.

This is the comment made by an engineer: 'The great word in engineering nowadays is "awareness" – awareness of people.' 'Awareness' – an engineering word? I thought awareness of people was a psychological or spiritual concept. Yet engineers are using the word because it seems right, and the reason it seems right is because it is right. This need not surprise us, as the whole universe was designed by God.

FURTHER STUDY

Luke 16:19–26; Acts 9:36–41

1. What was the rich man aware of?

2. What was Dorcas aware of?

A man who trains people in acting and public speaking wrote: 'The first thing you must learn in public speaking is not to think of your voice.' I am well aware that that is true because early in my ministry, when I was having difficulty with my throat, I was told: 'You are thinking too much of yourself. Think about others when you stand up to speak – what you can offer them and lead them into in the name of Christ.' I did, and the difference was quite remarkable.

Self-focus and self-concern is not-the-way. If you think of yourself you will become self-conscious; if you think of others you will become other-conscious. 'The Way' is written into our constitutions. We function better physically when we are more concerned about others than we are about ourselves.

God, when You made me, You made me for Your will and purposes. In them I live and move and have my being. Help me to look to the interests of others today. Amen.

Be a pacemaker

FOR READING & MEDITATION – JOHN 15:1–17

'If you obey my commands, you will remain in my love' (v10)

Today we conclude our meditations on the issues we need to consider and take on board if we are to go deeper with God. Permit me to remind you of them again. First, we are to cultivate an attitude of repentance. Our relationship with God begins through repentance and it is developed and deepened in the same way. Second, we make ourselves open to receiving God's grace. God is always eager to give us His grace... and there is so much of it. Third, we spend time with Him. We regularly read His Word, talk to Him in prayer, and make room in our devotions for Him to talk to us.

FURTHER STUDY

Col. 3:1–17;
1 John 2:6,
28; 3:6;
2 John 9

1. Where are we to set our hearts and minds?

2. What will be the result?

Fourth, we learn to be confident of His character. The great God who runs this universe can be trusted in everything. We cannot see from our perspective the good that underlies everything He does or allows, but we focus our gaze continually on the cross. There we see most clearly (and starkly) that God is love. Fifth, let's make it a priority to worship Him continually. He is worthy of our highest praise, and the more we worship Him the more we ourselves are drawn to health. For worship, as someone once put it, 'is inner health made audible'. Sixth, let's pursue Him with passion. Not just admire Him, but thirst after Him. Seventh, let's realise the importance of other-centred relationships remembering we are made in His image and for His glory. And, finally, we should seek out His way and walk obediently in it.

Commit yourselves to these things in the months and year ahead. If you do so, then there is no reason why you cannot keep pace with the most adventurous souls you know. In fact, without even knowing it, you may become a pacemaker as you pursue God and desire to see more of His glory.

Father, make this year a year of vision and adventure in the things of God. May it become a year of spiritual growth and depth I have never before known. I ask all this in Jesus' wonderful name. Amen.